WHAT THE SINGLE EYE SEES

WHAT THE SINGLE EYE SEES

Faith, Hope, Charity & the Pursuit of Discipleship

Dr. Joseph Q. Jarvis

This is a work of creative nonfiction. The events herein are portrayed to the best of the author's memory. While all the stories in this book are true, some names and identifying details may have been changed to protect the privacy of the people involved.

Editorial work and production management by Eschler Editing
Interior print design and layout by Marny K. Parkin.
eBook design and layout by Marny K. Parkin.

Published by Scrivener Books
ISBN 978-1-949165-06-7
First Edition: April 2019
Printed in the United States of America

To Annette W. Jarvis,
for whom I am humbly grateful

Contents

ACKNOWLEDGMENTS

I owe my most basic spiritual learning and understanding to the panoply of prophets, ancient and modern. I'm beyond grateful for scripture. In addition to these inspired voices are the many mentors I have enjoyed who have read scripture to me and talked with me about its meaning. My parents, Jarrett and Patricia Jarvis, were the first to do so. My mission president, Neil D Schaerrer, who like my father is deceased, followed thereafter. As did religion teachers at Brigham Young University, including Truman Madsen, who is also no longer in mortality. I owe many of the insights about faith, hope, and charity found in this book to conversations I had as a college student with my friend Paul D. Anderson. I'm extremely grateful for the editing skills of Kathy Jenkins, who made the manuscript flow, and Michele Preisendorf, who gave it her finishing touch of style perfection. Thanks also to Angela and her team at Eschler Editing and Chris Bigelow, of Scrivener Books, for their creative design and competent business approach in producing this book.

My Search for Jesus and His Grace

It was written that Joseph Smith is "arguably the most influential native-born figure in American religious history, and . . . almost certainly the most fascinating" (Margaret Salmon and Dean Wiand, "The Mormon Odyssey," *Newsweek*, Oct. 17, 2005). As a practicing member of The Church of Jesus Christ of Latter-day Saints, I number myself among those who admire Joseph Smith and have come to embrace his message. I agree with the *Newsweek* assessment that Joseph Smith—born in Vermont on December 23, 1805—is the most influential native-born American religious figure and a fascinating human being.

Fascinating as he is, this book is not another history of Joseph Smith. Rather, my purpose is to explore whether Joseph Smith achieved something he described in a letter dated January 4, 1833, addressed to N. E. Seaton, Esq., a newspaper editor in Rochester, New York. B. H. Roberts, a Church leader and historian of the early twentieth century, noted that Joseph Smith stated that this letter was written by commandment of God to serve as a warning to the inhabitants of the earth. Those people, as is stated in the letter's initial sentences, were suffering from the withdrawal of God's Holy Spirit (see *History of the Church*, 1:312). The third paragraph of the letter reads as follows:

> I think that it is high time for a Christian world to awake out of sleep, and cry mightily to that God, day and night, whose anger we have justly incurred. Are not these things a sufficient stimulant to arouse the faculties and call forth the energies of every man,

woman or child that possesses feelings of sympathy for their fellows, or that is in any degree endeared to the budding cause of our glorious Lord? I leave an intelligent community to answer this important question, with a confession, that this is what has caused me to overlook my own inability, and expose my weakness to a learned world; but, trusting in that God who has said that these things are hid from the wise and prudent and revealed unto babes, I step forth into the field to tell you what the Lord is doing, and what you must do, to enjoy the smiles of your Savior in these last days. (1:313)

I do not pretend to answer those questions as Joseph Smith himself would have, nor do I propose to offer the official views of the Church. I simply offer what I have learned and experienced as I have read about and tried to live a Christian life illuminated by Joseph Smith's teachings and prophecies. Simply, this book is my view of Christian discipleship.

Most of the chapters of this book were originally developed as sermons delivered over the pulpit during sacrament meeting. My feelings and thoughts about Christian discipleship originated over decades of serving as a home teacher and in various other callings. I am interested in explaining what Christ's call to discipleship means as I understand it in scripture (including the Bible) and as I have tried to live it among my neighbors, members of the Church and otherwise.

As the final writer in the Book of Mormon, Moroni outlived his entire civilization. Joseph Smith described meeting the angel Moroni, then a resurrected being, many times during the years 1823 to 1829, as Moroni prepared Joseph to translate that ancient record. Moroni advised Book of Mormon readers to "seek this Jesus of whom the prophets and apostles have written, that the grace of God the Father, and also the Lord Jesus Christ, and the Holy Ghost . . . may be and abide in you forever" (Ether 12:41). I hope to explain how Joseph Smith has helped me conduct my personal search for Jesus and His grace.

CALLED TO THE WORK

In early 1828, Martin Harris, a local farmer, began acting as scribe for the translation of the Book of Mormon. Joseph and Emma Smith had been married barely one year and were living on the property of her parents, Isaac and Alva Hale, in Harmony, Pennsylvania. Emma had previously been acting as scribe but was pregnant and less able to sit writing for long periods of time. Martin was therefore both needed as an assistant for translation and as a benefactor who had the resources to help the financially struggling young couple.

But Martin was also a doubter. At one point he secretly substituted a stone of his own for the "seer stone" Joseph had been using to do the translation. He was pleased when Joseph found that the substitute stone did not work.

Regardless, Martin and Joseph worked together steadily until June of 1828, at which time 116 pages of manuscript had been written. Martin repeatedly begged to be allowed to return to Palmyra, New York, with the manuscript, so he could read it to his wife. Eventually Joseph felt he had the Lord's approval for the errand.

Martin left for New York on June 14, 1828, with the only copy of the manuscript. Meanwhile, Joseph was caught up in the drama unfolding on the home front. Emma gave birth to an infant son the day after Martin left, but the baby died after living only a few hours, and Emma lay on the verge of death for two weeks. By July, when she was recovering, Joseph left her in the care of her parents and went in search of Martin Harris and the manuscript. But the manuscript had disappeared. The Lord chastised Joseph and Martin, and Joseph's privileges to translate were taken away.

Joseph returned to Harmony, where he worked on a small farm to support himself and Emma, who was still weak and recovering. It must have been a difficult winter for both of them. Joseph's parents did not hear from him for weeks over that winter. Likely motivated by concern for him and Emma, they traveled to Harmony in February 1829 to look in on them. (For details about this episode, refer to Donna Hill, *Joseph Smith: The First Mormon* [Signature Books, 1977]; or Richard L. Bushman, *Joseph Smith and the Beginnings of Mormonism* [University of Illinois Press, 1984]).

Joseph Smith Sr.'s questions about the work of God were answered with a revelation that ended a seven-month drought of communication from God for Joseph Jr. It is now known as section 4 of the Doctrine and Covenants. None of the subsequently published Book of Mormon had been translated by Joseph Smith before he dictated the following:

> Now behold, a marvelous work is about to come forth among the children of men.
>
> Therefore, O ye that embark in the service of God, see that ye serve him with all your heart, might, mind and strength, that ye may stand blameless before God at the last day.
>
> Therefore, if ye have desires to serve God ye are called to the work;
>
> For behold the field is white already to harvest; and lo, he that thrusteth in his sickle with his might, the same layeth up in store that he perisheth not, but bringeth salvation to his soul;
>
> And faith, hope, charity and love, with an eye single to the glory of God, qualify him for the work.
>
> Remember faith, virtue, knowledge, temperance, patience, brotherly kindness, godliness, charity, humility, diligence.
>
> Ask, and ye shall receive; knock, and it shall be opened unto you. Amen.

What would have been most obvious to Joseph Smith and his father about this paragraph—and what should be obvious to us—is the striking use of biblical references and imagery. Each sentence can be correlated to one or more Bible verses. This short revelation cannot be understood if its biblical roots are not explored. Christ's answer to Joseph Smith Sr.'s question came in words the young Prophet and his father were sure to understand because they knew the Bible. Today we can, and should, augment the biblical references with insights from scripture revealed through Joseph Smith subsequent to his receipt of section 4.

For instance, both father and son would have recognized the reference from Isaiah in the first verse about a "marvelous work." Isaiah explained that a marvelous work would be required because "people draw near [God] with their mouth" but "have removed their heart far from [Him]" (Isaiah 29:13). Isaiah further explained that the marvelous work included the publication of a book that a learned man could not read because it was sealed (see Isaiah 29:11).

Isaiah clarified that even though sealed, the book would do wonders: "And in that day shall the deaf hear the words of the book, and the eyes of the blind shall see out of obscurity, and out of darkness. The meek shall increase their joy in the Lord, and the poor among men shall rejoice in the Holy One of Israel. . . . They also that erred in spirit shall come to understanding, and they that murmured shall learn doctrine" (Isaiah 29:18–19, 24).

Nephi, one of Isaiah's most avid admirers, augmented the prophecies concerning this marvelous work. In the script Joseph later translated, Nephi wrote: "For the time cometh, saith the Lamb of God, that I will work a great and a marvelous work among the children of men; a work which shall be everlasting . . . either to the convincing of them unto peace and life eternal, or unto the deliverance of them to the hardness of their hearts and the blindness of their minds" (1 Nephi 14:7). According to Nephi, this marvelous work would commence among the Gentiles (those not originating from the land around Jerusalem), who would bring the house of Israel "out of captivity, . . . out of obscurity and out of darkness: and they shall know that the Lord is their Savior and their Redeemer, the Mighty One of Israel" (1 Nephi 22:12).

The book that could do such wonders is the Book of Mormon, which was "sealed by the hand of Moroni . . . ; to come forth . . . by way of the Gentiles—to the convincing of the Jew and Gentile that Jesus is the Christ" (Book of Mormon title page). This is the very book to which Joseph recommitted his time after receiving section 4. Because Joseph so desired, he was called to the work.

In the years since section 4 was given, ample evidence (for me, in any case) has accrued that God meant business when He asserted through His prophets that a marvelous work was to come forth. Despite tremendous odds, the Book of Mormon was published and has been the means of converting tens of millions of souls to Christ. I think it is fair to say that no explanation for the origins of the Book of Mormon other than the incredible one Joseph Smith offered has stood up to scrutiny. The Book of Mormon has been called one of the most influential books in American history, with five million copies acquired worldwide each year. Joseph Smith described the Book of Mormon as the keystone of The Church of Jesus Christ of Latter-day Saints and the book that could bring people nearer to God than any other. For me, that promise has come true.

It is truly a book of many wonders. Following are some of the wonders I find in the Book of Mormon:

- There is a remarkably accurate description of geographic features of the Arabian Peninsula, none of which would have been known in Joseph Smith's time. (See 1 Nephi)

- There are intimate descriptions of dysfunctional families. In fact, the Book of Mormon begins with the story of Lehi, whose sons hated each other. The sad tale of the breakup of this family seems written for modern people, many of whom come from disrupted families. (See 1 Nephi and 2 Nephi)

- The Bible states that we must each have faith, hope, and charity—but it is the Book of Mormon that teaches me what these are and how they can be acquired:

  ▸ There is no better scriptural description of faith than the one Alma gives in Alma 32. In that chapter we learn that faith is a loving relationship with Christ based on our own experimentation and consequent experience with His covenants.

‣ There is no better teacher of hope than Moroni, the man who lived what should have been a hopeless life, alone after all his people and family had been slaughtered. To Moroni, hope is an anchor for the soul, helping us see what is divine in each of us, keeping us from despair and pride. Moroni teaches us that hope is born in us by faith in Christ (see Moroni 7).

‣ Next to the Sermon on the Mount (which is also found in the Book of Mormon in 3 Nephi), there is no better sermon on charity than the one given by King Benjamin (see Mosiah 1–5). Those who study these two sermons will understand better what it means to love as God loves.

• The Book of Mormon teaches us how to understand and apply Isaiah's prophecies in our time.

• Lehi, preaches a sermon to his son Jacob about how to consecrate human suffering to our good; it is a remarkable summation of why people suffer and what they should do about it. (See 2 Nephi 2)

• In the Book of Mormon, a second scriptural witness for Christ, one can read about the Savior's response to a people who loved and appreciated what He did for them and said to them. The New Testament record of the Savior's life most often portrays Jesus engaged with people who actively opposed Him or were indifferent to Him. In the Book of Mormon, His preaching brings the audience to their knees in prayer and brings Jesus to a fullness of joy. (See 3 Nephi)

• There is no better statement, at least for me, about my condition and my spiritual needs than Nephi's statement in 2 Nephi 4, now often called Nephi's Psalm. It reads in part:

> Behold, my soul delighteth in the things of the Lord; and my heart pondereth continually upon the things which I have seen and heard.
>
> Nevertheless, notwithstanding the great goodness of the Lord, in showing me his great and marvelous works, my

heart exclaimeth: O wretched man that I am! Yea, my heart sorroweth because of my flesh; my soul grieveth because of my iniquities.

I am encompassed about, because of the temptations and the sins which do so easily beset me.

And when I desire to rejoice, my heart groaneth because of my sins; nevertheless, I know in whom I have trusted.

My God hath been my support; he hath led me through mine afflictions in the wilderness; and he hath preserved me upon the waters of the great deep.

He hath filled me with his love, even unto the consuming of my flesh.

He hath confounded mine enemies, unto the causing of them to quake before me.

Behold, he hath heard my cry by day, and he hath given me knowledge by visions in the night-time.

And by day have I waxed bold in mighty prayer before him; yea, my voice have I sent up on high; and angels came down and ministered unto me.

And upon the wings of his Spirit hath my body been carried away upon exceedingly high mountains. And mine eyes have beheld great things, yea, even too great for man; therefore I was bidden that I should not write them.

O then, if I have seen so great things, if the Lord in his condescension unto the children of men hath visited men in so much mercy, why should my heart weep and my soul linger in the valley of sorrow, and my flesh waste away, and my strength slacken, because of mine afflictions?

And why should I yield to sin, because of my flesh? Yea, why should I give way to temptations, that the evil one have place in my heart to destroy my peace and afflict my soul? Why am I angry because of mine enemy?

Awake, my soul! No longer droop in sin. Rejoice, O my heart, and give place no more for the enemy of my soul.

Do not anger again because of my enemies. Do not slacken my strength because of mine afflictions.

Rejoice, O my heart, and cry unto the Lord, and say: O Lord, I will praise thee forever; yea, my soul will rejoice in thee, my God, and the rock of my salvation. (2 Nephi 4:16–30)

- There is no better explanation about why we should regularly read the scriptures than that given by King Benjamin to his sons. He said that using scripture in our lives makes us spiritually literate, enables us to understand the mysteries of God, and constantly keeps the commandments of God before our eyes. The scriptures open up a world of beliefs for us to test. (See Mosiah 1)

- Finally, I love the Book of Mormon because in its pages I feel I really come to know, in a very personal way, the selected people whose writings were kept by Mormon in his abridgment. There are many examples of this personal touch, these voices from the dust who speak to the soul. Take as an example Jacob, Nephi's younger brother, who wrote: "And it came to pass that I, Jacob, began to be old; and the record of this people being kept on the other plates of Nephi, wherefore, I conclude this record, declaring that I have written according to the best of my knowledge, by saying that the time passed away with us, and also our lives passed away like as it were unto us a dream, we being a lonesome and a solemn people, wanderers, cast out from Jerusalem, born in tribulation, in a wilderness, and hated of our brethren, which caused wars and contentions; wherefore, we did mourn out our days" (Jacob 7:26).

The final six of the seven verses in section 4 of the Doctrine and Covenants deal with the only outstanding question about the marvelous work: Who, like Joseph Smith, will also do a marvelous work?

Section 4 is a pattern for Christian discipleship in the fullness of times. These words are meant for all of us who, like Joseph Smith Sr., wonder how we can help build the kingdom of God in the modern world.

The answer is surprisingly open-ended—"If ye have desires to serve God ye are called to the work" (D&C 4:3). It seems that whether you personally are called to participate in this work is very much up to you. I suppose it makes no sense to ask an unwilling person to serve—because, as Jesus said, "No man, having put his hand to the plough, and looking back, is fit for the kingdom of God" (Luke 9:62).

The plough has been offered to us if we have in our hearts a desire to grasp it. The calling is ours to take or leave. For His part, Jesus will pray that your desires lead you into this work: "But when he saw the multitudes, he was moved with compassion on them, because they fainted, and were scattered abroad, as sheep having no shepherd. Then saith he unto his disciples, The harvest truly is plenteous, but the labourers are few; Pray ye therefore the Lord of the harvest, that he will send forth labourers into his harvest" (Matthew 9:36–38). If your desires lead you to serve God, you are an answer to Christ's prayer.

Having a calling, of course, is not an end in itself. Section 4 states clearly what else we must do: "And faith, hope, charity and love, with an eye single to the glory of God, qualify him for the work" (D&C 4:5). If you want to proceed from desiring to serve God to being qualified for the work, you will exhibit faith, hope, charity (which is love), and an eye single to the glory of God.

"An eye single to the glory of God" is a statement about motivation. Service in God's kingdom cannot be motivated by anything that originates with us, such as guilt, goal setting, or desires for personal success in church work. We must be motivated as God is motivated. Two years after the dictation of section 4, Joseph learned what God had said to Moses about His (God's) motivation: "For behold, this is my work and my glory—to bring to pass the immortality and eternal life of man" (Moses 1:39). Our Father in Heaven is very single-minded. He does what it takes to bring His children back to be with Him and be like Him. We are qualified to share His work when we have the same sole motive.

Joseph Smith would have been schooled in the biblical Christian principles of faith, hope, and charity. He would have known that Paul said, "And now abideth faith, hope, and charity, these three" (1 Corinthians 13:13). At the time section 4 was revealed, however, he would not have known what Moroni had added: "Wherefore, if a man have faith he must needs have hope; . . . and . . . he cannot have faith and hope, save . . . he must needs have charity" (Moroni 7:42–44). Nor would Joseph learn until a few weeks later that Nephi taught that faith, hope, and charity are the crucial virtues necessary for a Christian to endure to the end of this life: "Wherefore, ye must press forward with a steadfastness in Christ, having a perfect brightness of hope, and a love of God and of all men" (2 Nephi 31:20).

Faith is what we call love of God, just as charity is the name for a love of God's children, our brothers and sisters. Hope is what a Christian thinks of themselves. Just as faith is found in reaching to God and His Son and charity is learned by reaching out to our brothers and sisters, so hope is realized by reaching into our own souls and finding there the image of Christ. We are not born into this world with these attributes; in fact, we are here to learn how to live by them. They do not come to us by chance but by our choice. We each have as much faith, hope, and charity as we make room for in our habits and character—they are gifts of God through the grace of His Son to the willing. They are the attributes of Christian discipleship and the fruits of a lifetime of obedience to Christ. When we finally have them, we are then qualified for Christ's work.

Once qualified, what harvest can we expect? What will be the promised blessings? "Therefore, O ye that embark in the service of God, see that ye serve him with all your heart, might, mind and strength, that ye may stand blameless before God at the last day. . . . For behold the field is white already to harvest; and lo, he that thrusteth in his sickle with his might, the same layeth up in store that he perisheth not, but bringeth salvation to his soul" (D&C 4:2, 4). In the end, service to God is about saving yourself.

Ammon and his brothers, all sons of King Mosiah and grandsons of King Benjamin, had joined Alma the Younger in persecuting the Nephite Christians. They, like Alma, were confronted about their egregious sins by an angel, sent to them by the prayers of their parents. With their repentance came a desire to forgo the opportunities of their royal birth because "they were desirous that salvation should be declared to every creature, for they could not bear that any human soul should perish" (Mosiah 28:3).

These men had desires for the work and were called to preach to their enemies, the Lamanites. They were motivated by what motivates God—their eyes were single. The Lord told them how to go about their work: "Be patient in long-suffering and afflictions, that ye may show forth good examples unto them in me" (Alma 17:11).

Ammon entered the land of Ishmael and was taken prisoner before Lamanite king Lamoni, who took a liking to Ammon and offered him a daughter to marry. Ammon refused the royal life a second time and asked instead to be a servant. He was assigned to the flocks, where he encountered an opportunity for valiant service. But to King Lamoni, the most impressive thing about Ammon's service was that, after saving the flock, Ammon simply went on with his chores, feeding the horses: "Now when king Lamoni heard that Ammon was preparing his horses . . . he was more astonished, because of the faithfulness of Ammon, saying: surely there has not been any servant among all my servants that has been so faithful as this man; for even he doth remember all my commandments to execute them" (Alma 18:10).

It was as if Ammon had read verse 6 in section 4 and had followed it to the letter: "Remember faith, virtue, knowledge, temperance, patience, brotherly kindness, godliness, charity, humility, diligence." Ammon was a competent and caring servant to a king who was accustomed only to incompetence and avarice, and the contrast was sermon enough to astonish the king, who then opened his heart to the message.

Ammon sums up the fruit of his labors: "Now if this is boasting, even so will I boast; for this is my life and my light, my joy and my salvation, and my redemption from everlasting wo. Yea, blessed is the name of my God, who has been mindful of this people, wanderers in a strange land" (Alma 26:36).

I see a marvelous work coming forth among the children of men. Joseph Smith, at the direction of God, desired and was called to the work of translating and publishing the Book of Mormon. It is now available in more than one hundred languages with one hundred million copies printed. The marvelous work is happening—the only question is whether I will participate in it.

How do I get the message of that book so that when I err in spirit I can still come to understanding? Section 4 spells it out. I will participate in the marvelous work if I have desires to serve like Ammon did, putting the kingdom of God before anything of this earth. Then, if I am motivated by the same thing that motivates God, I will put my desires to serve into the greatest cause on earth: "to bring to pass the immortality and eternal life of men." Being so motivated, I will spend my might, mind, and strength acquiring faith, hope, and charity. I will discover, as did Ammon, that the greatest sermons are those I deliver by doing well what assignments I am given—in my home, my neighborhood, my children's schools, and among all of my brothers and sisters. I will be found doing the chores, like Ammon as he was feeding the horses, with humility, patience, and diligence.

THE WHITE FIELD

When Jesus was at the well in Samaria, He testified to the woman drawing water there that He was the Messiah and Jehovah of the Old Testament. As she left to tell her fellow townspeople about the Christ who had come to town, His disciples returned with provisions and begged Him to eat something. He refused, knowing that He would very soon be teaching many townspeople, explaining to his friends,

> My meat is to do the will of him that sent me, and to finish his work.
>
> Say not ye, There are yet four months, and then cometh harvest? behold, I say unto you, Lift up your eyes, and look on the fields; for they are white already to harvest.
>
> And he that reapeth receiveth wages, and gathereth fruit unto life eternal: that both he that soweth and he that reapeth may rejoice together.
>
> And herein is that saying true, One soweth, and another reapeth.
>
> I sent you to reap that whereon ye bestowed no labour: other men laboured, and ye are entered into their labours." (John 4:34–38)

The metaphor of comparing people ready to hear the gospel message to a field ready to harvest captured John's imagination with its simplicity, and he included it in his Gospel, written many decades later.

Many centuries later, as Jesus was preparing to restore His gospel and Church on earth, He answered Joseph Smith Sr.'s question by employing the same metaphor about serving God: "For behold the field is white already to harvest; and lo, he that thrusteth in his sickle with his might, the same layeth up in store that he perisheth not, but bringeth salvation to his soul" (D&C 4:4).

Both the Prophet Joseph Smith and his father would have recognized the reference to the Savior's words spoken at the well in Samaria. They would have realized, being farmers themselves, that the harvest is an urgent event; no delay is possible. Ripe grain harvested late may spoil. They also would have understood that the harvest required a commitment of all available resources to the fields. Anything less risked delay and crop loss. The farmer's family makes this total commitment no matter the inconvenience because they know that their own lives are at stake. Maximum effort at harvest yields maximum food storage for the farmer and his family.

By reusing His Samaritan harvest metaphor in answering Joseph Smith Sr.'s question about serving God, Christ emphasizes that there are important parallels between farming and service to God in the latter days. There are seasons or times when we may recognize that a nearby gospel field is white already to harvest. By virtue of a specific calling or simply by living among our neighbors, we may see a need that should be met. A true servant of God is always in the field, prepared to reap where others have sown. These efforts, like the harvest of grain, may be required at the cost of inconvenience, discomfort, or difficulty. When an opportunity for specific service to God presents itself, we may have to forgo a meal, sleep, or entertainment. We should consider these opportunities as moments of harvest, needing the focus, urgency, and all-out effort of a field of ripened grain.

I am persuaded that Joseph Smith and his father both understood what Jesus intended with the harvest metaphor. The meaning is probably less obvious to those readers of this revelation who do not have any agricultural experience.

But it was not just the physical effort of the harvest, the sickle thrust with might, that was required of the servant of God: "Therefore, O ye that embark in the service of God, see that ye serve him with all your heart, might, mind and strength, that ye may stand blameless before God at the last day" (D&C 4:2). People doing hard physical labor may give it their whole physical capacity, their might and strength, without either thinking about the work or caring much for it. But those who embark in the service of God are not joining a labor camp. They are asked to think clearly and feel wholeheartedly about this work.

King David made this same point to his son Solomon when he charged him before all Israel to build the temple, the footstool of God and resting place for the ark of the covenant: "And thou, Solomon my son, know thou the God of thy father, and serve him with a perfect heart and with a willing mind: for the Lord searcheth all hearts, and understandeth all the imaginations of the thoughts: if thou seek him, he will be found of thee; but if thou forsake him, he will cast thee off for ever. Take heed now; for the Lord hath chosen thee to build an house for the sanctuary: be strong, and do it" (1 Chronicles 28:9–10). Like Solomon, we have a task given us of God; like him, we must come with perfect hearts and willing minds and do it.

A willing mind listens to the Lord; such a person has the ears to hear (see Matthew 11:15), to which Jesus often referred. A willing mind will always think about God, will always remember Him, as I promise to do each week when I partake of the sacrament (see D&C 20:77). A willing mind will confess God's hand in all things (see D&C 59:21). "Neither be ye of doubtful mind" (Luke 12:29), Christ instructed His disciples, meaning that the intellectually honest accept the uncertainty of this life as a basis for faith, not doubt. We should choose our questions carefully and then "seek learning, even by study and also by faith" (D&C 88:118).

So that Joseph Smith and his colleague Oliver Cowdery would be clear about the need to apply their minds to God's service, Christ made an unmistakable statement two months after He revealed section 4: "Behold, you have not understood; you have supposed that I would give it unto you, when you took no thought save it was to ask me. But, behold, I say unto you, that you must study it out in your mind; then you must ask me if it be right, and if it is right I will cause that your bosom shall burn within you; therefore, you shall feel that it is right. But if it be not right you shall have no such feelings, but you shall have a stupor of thought that shall cause you to forget the thing which is wrong" (D&C 9:7–9). God does not do our thinking for us. What we can learn or reason by our own efforts He leaves to us to discover. If we are too lazy to learn how to manage our personal resources or appreciate fine art or apply good science to our lives, we will be left to the consequences of our mistakes, and we will be that much less able to serve God.

Our efforts to expand our minds in this life will carry over to the next: "Whatever principle of intelligence we attain unto in this life, it will rise with us in the resurrection. And if a person gains more knowledge and intelligence in this life through his diligence and obedience than another, he will have so much the advantage in the world to come" (D&C 130:18–19). There is a direct correlation between the exercise of intellectual capacity and success in this and the next life. Reason can change fanaticism to faith. Every man and woman striving to serve God should seek the highest education possible. This is what it means to serve God with all your mind.

To serve God with all your heart requires a different kind of training. We are instructed in Proverbs that "he that trusteth in his own heart is a fool" (28:26). This may seem like a harsh assessment of our natural feelings—those things that are commonly in the hearts of men. Paul told the Corinthians that he could not speak spiritually to them because they were still carnal: "For whereas there is among you envying, and strife, and divisions, are ye not carnal, and walk as men?" (1 Corinthians 3:3). The implication is that these newly converted Saints were allowing the foibles of human nature to interfere with their spiritual growth; they remained yet too concerned about wanting what they did not have.

In his letter to the Romans, Paul touched on the same theme: "For they that are after the flesh do mind the things of the flesh; but they that are after the Spirit the things of the Spirit. For to be carnally minded is death; but to be spiritually minded is life and peace. Because the carnal mind is enmity against God: for it is not subject to the law of God, neither indeed can be. So then they that are in the flesh cannot please God" (Romans 8:5–8).

In King Benjamin's words, "For the natural man is an enemy to God, and has been from the fall of Adam, and will be, forever and ever, unless he yields to the enticings of the Holy Spirit, and putteth off the natural man and becometh a saint through the atonement of Christ the Lord, and becometh as a child, submissive, meek, humble, patient, full of love, willing to submit to all things which the Lord seeth fit to inflict upon him, even as a child doth submit to his father" (Mosiah 3:19).

I don't think that King Benjamin or Paul implied in any way that humans by nature are hated by God. In fact, King Benjamin points out that little children are born with characteristics adults should emulate. Children desire to please their parents; their hearts are prepared to receive instruction from their elders. As we grow older, however, our hearts may be captured by the desires, appetites, and passions awakened by the stimulations and attractions of our physical bodies and the offerings of a fallen world. King Benjamin's "natural man" is the carnally minded person in Paul's epistles; they both are God's enemies. People in this awful position are, as Paul said, "lovers of their own selves, covetous, boasters, proud, blasphemers, disobedient to parents, unthankful, unholy, without natural affection, trucebreakers, false accusers, incontinent, fierce, despisers of those that are good, traitors, heady, highminded, lovers of pleasures more than lovers of God; having a form of godliness, but denying the power thereof" (2 Timothy 3:2–5).

The people Paul describes, as Joseph Smith later revealed, are called but not chosen "because their hearts are set so much upon the things of this world, and aspire to the honors of men" (D&C 121:35) that their minds cannot learn heavenly lessons. As Christ pointed out, your heart will be where your treasure is (see Matthew 6:21). If what we treasure most is something of this world, if our hearts are set on having success with a worldly pursuit, our lives will be spent achieving our carnal ambitions. Inevitably a crush on carnal things will alienate us from God; we cannot serve two masters.

Exactly this loss of spiritual opportunity is anticipated in the parable of the sower, as found in the Gospel of Luke. In that parable, the seeds that fall among thorns "are they, which, when they have heard, go forth, and are choked with cares and riches and pleasures of this life, and bring no fruit to perfection. But that on the good ground are they, which in an honest and good heart, having heard the word, keep it, and bring forth fruit with patience" (Luke 8:14–15).

The word of God is the same to all; those who are blessed by the word of God are those whose hearts are prepared. When your heart is prepared, you can be prepared for your ultimate encounter with Christ, who said: "And take heed to yourselves, lest at any time your hearts be overcharged with surfeiting, and drunkenness, and cares of this life, and so that day come upon you unawares" (Luke 21:34).

Paul teaches that the desires of the heart determine the direction of the mind:

> This I say therefore, and testify in the Lord, that ye henceforth walk not as other Gentiles walk, in the vanity of their mind,
>
> Having the understanding darkened, being alienated from the life of God through the ignorance that is in them, because of the blindness of their heart:
>
> Who being past feeling have given themselves over unto lasciviousness, to work all uncleanness with greediness.
>
> But ye have not so learned Christ;
>
> If so be that ye have heard him, and have been taught by him, as the truth is in Jesus:
>
> That ye put off concerning the former conversation the old man, which is corrupt according to the deceitful lusts;
>
> And be renewed in the spirit of your mind;
>
> And that ye put on the new man, which after God is created in righteousness and true holiness. (Ephesians 4:17–24)

A blind heart creates an unfeeling, greedy person whose understanding is darkened. Such a person is ignorant of spiritual things and alienated from life with God. The truth taught and lived by Jesus exposes the deceit inherent in lust and thereby renews the mind, making possible the creation of a new person who is created by God in righteousness and holiness.

This process of ridding one's heart of worldly passions requires significant, often painful, effort. As recorded by Joel, "Therefore also now, saith the Lord, turn ye even to me with all your heart, and with fasting, and with weeping, and with mourning: and rend your heart, and not your garments, and turn unto the Lord your God: for he is gracious and merciful, slow to anger, and of great kindness" (Joel 2:12–13).

When a young man has a crush on a girl and she spurns him, we say that she has broken his heart. The end of a romance is often painful; the object of affection must be removed from one's heart and replaced with something else. It can be the case that we know intellectually that we must give up a strong attraction to someone or something because that attraction is not good for us—but despite what we know, we continue to have feelings of longing for the object of our passion.

People can go through the motions of doing what they know to be right, but if their heart is not in the effort, they will ultimately fail to accomplish their proper goal. That is why Joel tells the people of his era that they must rend or break their hearts of their worldly passions and not just go through the motions of sorrow by rending their garments. Mormon, the father of Moroni and ancient editor of the book that bears his name, likewise observed that people in his era were sorry—not to repentance, but because "the Lord would not always suffer them to take happiness in sin . . . they did not come unto Jesus with broken hearts and contrite spirits, but they did curse God, and wish to die. Nevertheless they would struggle with the sword for their lives" (Mormon 2:13–14). It was Mormon who really sorrowed as he saw his brothers and sisters without grace and killed by the thousands "in open rebellion against their God" (Mormon 2:15).

The hard line between filling our hearts with the things of God while removing from our affections the things of this world was starkly taught to Peter by Jesus Himself:

From that time forth began Jesus to shew unto his disciples, how that he must go unto Jerusalem, and suffer many things of the elders and chief priests and scribes, and be killed, and be raised again the third day.

Then Peter took him, and began to rebuke him, saying, Be it far from thee, Lord: this shall not be unto thee.

But he turned, and said unto Peter, Get thee behind me, Satan: thou art an offence unto me: for thou savourest not the things that be of God, but those that be of men.

Then said Jesus unto his disciples, If any man will come after me, let him deny himself, and take up his cross, and follow me.

For whosoever will save his life shall lose it: and whosoever will lose his life for my sake shall find it.

For what is a man profited, if he shall gain the whole world, and lose his own soul? or what shall a man give in exchange for his soul? (Matthew 16:21–26)

Peter's fault was that he preferred that Jesus not suffer at the hands of the chief priests, even if that meant that the Resurrection would not happen. All of us are naturally inclined to shun a course that will clearly bring us misery and suffering, but if the price for avoiding pain is our eternal salvation, we must give up our longing for ease and get on with accepting our cross. What worldly comfort is worth exchanging for our soul? We are commanded by God to sacrifice of ourselves: "Thou shalt offer a sacrifice unto the Lord thy God in righteousness, even that of a broken heart and a contrite spirit" (D&C 59:8).

So the harvest we should reap begins within us. For as Jeremiah wrote, "Behold, the days come, saith the Lord, that I will sow the house of Israel and the house of Judah with the seed of man. . . . So will I watch over them, to build, and to plant, saith the Lord. . . . I will make a new covenant with the house of Israel, and with the house of Judah: . . . I will put my law in their inward parts, and write it in their hearts; and will be their God, and they shall be my people" (Jeremiah 31:27–28, 31, 33).

Joseph Smith believed that the people who accept the Book of Mormon are the people of Jeremiah's prophecy, the people of the new covenant. Of these people "the Lord requireth the heart and a willing mind; and the willing and obedient shall eat the good of the land of Zion in these last days" (D&C 64:34). "Therefore," revealed Joseph Smith to his father, "O ye that embark in the service of God, see that ye serve him with all your heart, might, mind and strength, that ye may stand blameless before God at the last day. . . . For behold the field is white already to harvest; and lo, he that thrusteth in his sickle with his might, the same layeth up in store that he perisheth not, but bringeth salvation to his soul" (D&C 4:2, 4). We are the grain ready to harvest; service to God is what saves our souls.

FAITH

THE FIRST PRINCIPLE OF THE GOSPEL

In the Gospel of Mark, we find the interesting story of a man sick with palsy who was healed by Jesus. At the time of the healing, Jesus was in a house in Capernaum. The house was filled with so many people that there was no room for anyone to move. As four men carried the sick man on a bed, it was impossible for them to get into the house through the door—so they climbed up on the house, broke the roof, and lowered the bed into the room where Jesus stood. Mark then records that when "Jesus saw their faith," he healed the sick man and forgave him his sins (Mark 2:5).

What did Jesus see that confirmed the faith of these men?

Faith is the first principle of the gospel of Jesus Christ. On this point, all prophets are unanimous. Through Moses, Jehovah declared, "I am the Lord thy God, which have brought thee out of the land of Egypt, out of the house of bondage. Thou shalt have no other gods before me" (Exodus 20:2–3). And as Jesus, the mortal Son of God on earth, He restated: "Thou shalt love the Lord thy God with all thy heart, and with all thy soul, and with all thy mind. This is the first and great commandment" (Matthew 22:37–38). This relationship of love with God, which is faith, is placed first because all blessings flow from it. Faith precedes repentance. Faith is the premise of all spiritual gifts. Faith makes salvation possible.

One of the most compelling examples of faith is Elijah. There is no book by Elijah in the Old Testament; we know him principally by his deeds. His name means "My God is Jehovah," and that alone would have made him a marked man in a time when belief in a single god was under threat of extinction. There were only a few thousand believers in Jehovah remaining in either the kingdom of Judah or the Northern Kingdom of Israel when Elijah began his ministry by sealing the heavens and defying the worshipers of Baal, the supposed god of rain.

More than anything else, it was Elijah's connection to the Spirit of God that enabled him to reach the hearts of the house of Israel and teach them faith in the living God. He was the greatest prophet of Israel between Moses and Jesus, which accounts for his appearance both on the Mount of Transfiguration and in the Kirtland Temple. When the time came for him to end his earthly ministry, Elisha, his successor, was right there with him: "And it came to pass . . . that Elijah said unto Elisha, Ask what I shall do for thee, before I be taken away from thee. And Elisha said, I pray thee, let a double portion of thy spirit be upon me" (2 Kings 2:9). Elisha had been at his teacher's side and therefore knew how the work of God moved forward. He also knew that he could succeed only if he too was blessed with the Spirit of God. So "He took up also the mantle of Elijah that fell from him, and went back, and stood by the bank of Jordan; And he took the mantle of Elijah that fell from him, and smote the waters, and said, Where is the Lord God of Elijah?" (2 Kings 2:13–14).

It seems to me that we are more like Elisha than perhaps we generally understand. We too are living in a time when monotheism—the belief in one god—is under threat of extinction. There are but few on the earth today who worship the true and living God of Abraham, Isaac, and Jacob.

In our dispensation there has also been a mighty Prophet who has made it possible for us to connect ourselves to the work of salvation through the Spirit of God. We as Latter-day Saints have seen the mantle of prophet fall from Joseph Smith's shoulders onto his several successors, including our current living prophet. We, like Elisha, are standing at the Jordan River with the task of a lifetime ahead of us on the other side of the river. Like Elisha, we must ask for a double portion of the Spirit of God, and then call out, "Where is the Lord God of Joseph Smith?"

Unlike Elijah, Joseph Smith wrote many revelations, scriptures, instructions, and teachings in which we can find an answer to this question. By revelation to Joseph Smith, the Lord clearly identified what was happening to the faith of the family of man right at the time Joseph began to build the kingdom of God on earth. Speaking of all people around the world in 1831, He said:

> For they have strayed from mine ordinances, and have broken mine everlasting covenant;
>
> They seek not the Lord to establish his righteousness, but every man walketh in his own way, and after the image of his own god, whose image is in the likeness of the world, and whose substance is that of an idol . . .
>
> Wherefore, I the Lord, knowing the calamity which should come upon the inhabitants of the earth, called upon my servant Joseph Smith, Jun., and spake unto him from heaven, and gave him commandments." (D&C 1:15–17)

The calamity of losing a collective faith in God and replacing Him with an image in the likeness of the world happened over a fifty-year time span in the late eighteenth and early nineteenth centuries. Joseph Smith was born at the beginning of that fifty-year period of time during which most of the citizens of the Western world lost their faith in Christianity. Faith was replaced with agnosticism, atheism, and superstition. The world, which had previously appeared so beautiful and new, appeared from then on to be a place without joy, love, light, certitude, peace, or help for pain. This was the calamity God knew would happen and to which He responded by calling on Joseph Smith.

The effects of this calamity are felt throughout the Church, including in our own neighborhoods. As ward mission leader for three years, I worked weekly with the missionaries, tracting, teaching investigators, visiting the homes of every person not assigned a home teacher, and arranging to knock on the doors of most people living in the ward boundaries who were not members of the Church. I met people in many different states of belief—they walked in their own way, after the image of their own god. These are the people both Alma the Younger and Paul designated as "without God in the world" (Alma 41:11; Ephesians 2:12).

Paul added that such people are "without Christ, being aliens from the commonwealth of Israel, and strangers from the covenants of promise, having no hope" (Ephesians 2:12).

God's response to the calamity of failing faith was to command Joseph Smith to restore priesthood authority, increase faith, establish covenants, and bring the fullness of the gospel to the entire world.

This is merely the work Jesus began when He established His earthly ministry.

When asked which is the first commandment, Jesus declared: "Thou shalt love the Lord thy God with all thy heart, and with all thy soul, and with all thy mind" (Matthew 22:37). After Alma taught how to gain faith, Amulek taught in whom to have faith: "We have beheld that the great question which is in your minds is whether the word be in the Son of God, or whether there shall be no Christ" (Alma 34:5).

That great question remains an open one for billions of people on the earth today, including those affiliated with Christian denominations. Their faith is not increasing because they do not understand that faith is a love of God and His Son, Jesus Christ—nor do they understand the nature of God the Father and His Only Begotten. There has been an enduring debate in the Christian world about whether God is transcendent or personal, one entity or three, caring or indifferent.

Because God's nature seems mystical, not understandable, not describable in human words, faith has become mysterious, blind, passive, superstitious, and more like guesswork. Assuming faith is passive makes an increase in faith impossible. Assuming God is not describable makes God unavailable for a loving relationship.

Joseph Smith's First Vision wipes away all of these false assumptions about God and faith. Said President Gordon B. Hinckley: "In this divine revelation there was reaffirmed beyond doubt the reality of the literal resurrection of the Lord Jesus Christ. This knowledge of Deity, hidden from the world for centuries, was the first and great thing which God revealed to His chosen servant" ("The Great Things Which God Has Revealed," Conference Report, April 2005).

The knowledge given in the First Vision made it possible for faith to increase in the earth. Because faith is the first principle, nothing spiritual can happen in the lives of our neighbors until their faith begins to increase, until they begin to know God well enough to love Him.

For many people today who lack faith, the command to have faith seems an impossible task. From their perspective, they are told that without faith they can do nothing spiritual, yet they must be spiritual in order to have faith. To these people, faith seems to require a blind leap—they must close their eyes to what they know and experience and hope that something else takes its place.

I have seen some Church materials define faith as an unquestioning belief. During my mission service in Austria as a young man, one of the people I contacted explained his refusal to listen to a gospel message by stating that he envied the gift of faith I had but recognized he had not been given that gift. In essence, faith appeared to him to be wishful thinking, and he figured that some just had a capacity to wish harder than others.

Many living during the rise of modern science feel that the wishful thinking of religion is outdated. For them, the answers to life's questions are found in science. For proof, they point out that we know so much more about the material reality of the universe than was the case when Christianity began. Science compels them to give up faith because of what they know. Paul's definition of faith makes no sense to them; there is no substance for things only hoped for and no credible evidence unless it is seen or somehow detected (see Hebrews 11:1). People of our age can enjoy fiction with a willing suspension of disbelief, but they find a permanent suspension of disbelief not just impossible but purposeless. Many modern people claim to be unbelieving because science has made faith unnecessary.

Science can even explain how some are tricked into believing something. Charles Dickens wrote about being tricked into belief in *A Christmas Carol*. Just after Scrooge encounters Marley's ghost, an interesting dialogue takes place between Scrooge and the ghost:

"You don't believe in me," observed the Ghost.

"I don't," said Scrooge.

"What evidence would you have of my reality beyond that of your own senses?"

"I don't know," said Scrooge.

"Why do you doubt your senses?"

"Because," said Scrooge, "a little thing affects them. A slight disorder of the stomach makes them cheats. You may be an undigested bit of beef, a blot of mustard, a crumb of cheese, a fragment of an underdone potato. There's more of gravy than of grave about you, whatever you are!" ...

At this the spirit raised a frightful cry, and shook its chain. ...

Scrooge fell upon his knees, and clasped his hands before his face.

"Mercy!" he said. "Dreadful apparition, why do you trouble me?"

"Man of the worldly mind!" replied the Ghost, "do you believe in me or not?"

"I do," said Scrooge, "I must." (London: Bradbury and Evans, 1858, 17–18)

Whenever I see that scene replayed, I am reminded of an episode from my own life as a high school senior. One of my teachers was a modern nonbeliever, a man of a "worldly mind." My classmates were virtually all raised by parents with Judeo-Christian beliefs. Our teacher had a reputation for provoking his students to debate him about the existence of God and then, with sarcasm, humiliating them into silent defeat. We all feared this outcome and resisted his daily entreaties to discuss Deity. Ultimately I grew tired of his harangue, though, and I became curious about the reasons for his unbelief. One day I responded to his invitation and asked him to explain his atheism. His answer was that any god worth his salt would not leave the world in such chaos about religion. "If God exists," he asked, "why doesn't He come down to the classroom and put the controversy to rest?" My teacher wanted a Scrooge experience. He wanted the equivalent of Marley's ghost to come to him and compel his faith.

We are taught by Moses that such an alternative was discussed in the premortal existence and rejected: "[Satan] came before [God] saying—Behold, here am I, send me, I will be thy son, and I will redeem all mankind, that one soul shall not be lost" (Moses 4:1). Satan's plan would have eliminated the messiness of competing beliefs among men; Satan proposed to overwhelm each of us, like Marley's ghost, into a correct religion.

No matter how ugly, chaotic, and violent the confusion about belief is in this life, it is nothing short of a miracle that we are free to believe whatever we choose. Somehow, God created this world and our physical capabilities to appreciate the splendor of it, planted the Light of Christ (see Moroni 7:15, 18, 19) in our minds, and still left room for us to doubt His very existence. He does not ruin the miracle by going about like Marley's ghost to settle doubt and debate. As Lehi taught his sons, "Wherefore the Lord God gave unto man that he should act for himself. Wherefore, man could not act for himself save it should be that he was enticed by the one or the other" (2 Nephi 2:16).

There are at least two consequences that follow our freedom to believe whatever we will. First, we must believe something. As Paul said, "For now we see through a glass, darkly" (1 Corinthians 13:12)—which is to say, this life is an enigma; the full truth is not revealed to any of us. Most people today, just as the Athenians to whom Paul preached on Mars Hill, ignorantly worship or believe something, often choosing something "gold, or silver, or stone, graven by art and man's device" (Acts 17:29). For example, the sciences are a human device, built upon a man-made way of thinking about the world. Science is clever, useful, and can be beneficial, but it is not an escape from the requirement to believe since, at its core, science requires us to accept a metaphor.

The second consequence of our freedom to believe is that what we choose to believe matters a lot. Superstitious people believe in fate or astrology or lady luck and tend to live passive lives of acceptance. Why act if you believe that your actions make no difference? The concept that well-chosen beliefs stimulate people to action that brings reward has been taught for millennia. Socrates said that the unexamined life is not worth living.

Thoreau would have agreed; he said that the mass of men lived lives of quiet desperation not because they had to but because they chose their beliefs poorly. The scriptures are full of instruction about how to properly choose belief. There are fifty references to belief in the Gospel of John alone.

What the scriptures clearly teach is that anyone can have faith, because everyone has a choice about what he or she believes, and well-chosen beliefs lead to faith. Alma puts it most bluntly: "But behold, if ye will awake and arouse your faculties, even to an experiment upon my words, and exercise a particle of faith, yea, even if ye can no more than desire to believe, let this desire work in you, even until ye believe in a manner that ye can give place for a portion of [God's] words" (Alma 32:27). Even just a *desire* to believe is the beginning of faith; Alma is pleading with us to just give the word of God a try. He compares this word to a seed and promises that if we just try it out in our heart and take care of it, it will grow and we will feel it "enlarge" the soul, enlighten the understanding, and taste delicious. This, Alma says, will strengthen and increase faith.

Amulek, Alma's missionary companion in spiritual work, drives home the lesson about what seed to plant: "The great question which is in your minds is whether the word be in the Son of God, or whether there shall be no Christ" (Alma 34:5). Everyone can ask that question. Everyone can desire to believe in Christ's power to free us from sin. And everyone can experiment with that desire to see how good the grace of God can be.

Abraham is a prime example of a man who asked the right questions and followed through to find the answers. He desired happiness, peace, rest, instruction, and knowledge. But he was surrounded by people who chose to worship in an ignorant and unthinkable way. They worshiped tangible objects made by their own devices. Abraham desired to believe that there was something more than acquiescence to superstition. He would have listened to King Benjamin, who counseled, "Believe in God; believe that he is, and that he created all things, both in heaven and in earth; believe that he has all wisdom, and all power, both in heaven and in earth; believe that man doth not comprehend all the things which the Lord can comprehend" (Mosiah 4:9).

But the ruler of Abraham's country was unrighteous and sought to destroy Abraham. Abraham experimented with his desire to believe, called upon God, and was saved. Then he was twice directed to leave his home and go to an unknown place. Abraham's response is a classic example of how to awake and arouse your faculties to experiment with God's word: "I [Abraham] said in my heart: Thy servant has sought thee earnestly; now I have found thee . . . and I will do well to hearken unto thy voice, therefore let thy servant rise up and depart in peace. . . . Therefore, eternity was our covering and our rock and our salvation" (Abraham 2:12–16).

An experiment requires that we make an effort to try something different. For Abraham, it was a journey to a new home; for us, it may be reading scripture, learning a new doctrine, or obeying a commandment more thoroughly. The alternative is to believe that nothing can ever change, that no happiness or peace is possible, that our life can't improve. Why not at least desire to believe that God can help us do better? Abraham not only carried out the experiment, he periodically checked in with God through prayer. He stopped twice on his journey from Haran to Canaan to build an altar, offer sacrifice, and call on the Lord devoutly.

Since faith is a relationship with God, it makes sense that the development of faith would require a means for conversation with God. Of course, we pray to ask God for help with our experiment in belief. But a prayer is never properly begun without a statement of gratitude. As revealed by Joseph Smith, "And in nothing doth man offend God, or against none is his wrath kindled, save those who confess not his hand in all things" (D&C 59:21).

Like Abraham, any person who desires something more in this life and is willing to try to get it by experimenting with God's word can start by giving God something that God otherwise would not have: gratitude. You properly start your relationship with God by acknowledging His hand in all things—by recognizing what God has already done for you.

For those unpracticed in giving thanks to God, I recommend a scripture that provides prophetic statements of gratitude. Said the Psalmist:

Make a joyful noise unto the Lord, all ye lands.

Serve the Lord with gladness: Come before his presence with singing.

Know ye that the Lord he is God: it is he that hath made us, and not we ourselves; we are his people, and the sheep of his pasture.

Enter into his gates with thanksgiving, and into his courts with praise: be thankful unto him, and bless his name.

For the Lord is good; his mercy is everlasting; and his truth endureth to all generations. (Psalm 100:1–5)

In these verses is the seed Alma spoke of—the particle of faith, the mere desire that can begin each person's spiritual journey toward faith.

Each of us must believe something about this life. For instance, we may choose to believe we are creatures of a pitiless nature, begotten with enough consciousness to know that matter and energy are conserved but our identity is not. Or we can choose to believe (or desire to believe) that God made us and that all of us are God's people, the sheep of His pasture, blessed by His truth, goodness, and mercy.

And if we choose to be thankful, we are blessed in more ways, as revealed by Joseph Smith: "And inasmuch as ye do these things with thanksgiving . . . the fulness of the earth is yours . . . all things which come of the earth . . . are made for the benefit and the use of man, both to please the eye and to gladden the heart; yea for food and for raiment, for taste and for smell, to strengthen the body and enliven the soul. And it pleaseth God that he hath given all these things unto man" (D&C 59:15–21).

Gratitude is a catalyst by which we accelerate our apprehension and enjoyment of this earth. By choosing to be grateful, we live more fully with our senses and are more alive in our soul. And when more fully alive, we are more pleasing to God. When we choose to be grateful to God, we change our relationship with God.

Those who fail in their experiment on God's word often do so because of ingratitude. Paul the Apostle said: "Because that, when they knew God, they glorified him not as God, neither were thankful; but became vain in their imaginations, and their foolish heart was darkened. Professing themselves to be wise, they became fools, and changed the glory of the uncorruptible God into an image made like to corruptible man, and to birds, and fourfooted beasts, and creeping things." (Romans 1:21–23)

People who choose not to thank God, as Paul points out, are a mere step away from replacing God in their hearts and minds with the corruptions and foolishness of this world. If we are not giving God the meager thanks that we have, we are giving them to someone or something else. After the children of Israel were mercifully brought out of slavery in Egypt by the hand of almighty God, they lost their focus on God and His daily gifts of prophecy, protection, and provenance; they had no thanksgiving because they could think only of their arduous journey. No wonder they soon refused to look upon God. They sent Moses alone to encounter Him, and while Moses was away, they foolishly worshiped a man-made image. Through ingratitude, a whole generation of Israelites gave away their chance to enjoy the fullness of the gospel. Instead, they became a generation ever traveling and never reaching the promised land.

The children of Israel should have followed the example of their father Abraham. He regularly made gifts of gratitude and paid tithes and offerings. By doing so, he transitioned from one who merely desired to believe to a man of great faith—in other words, he was a man who knew and loved God and who participated with God in fulfilling a divine purpose here on earth.

Faith is a partnership with our Father in Heaven. And the partnership goes both ways, for as God said of Abraham, "For I know [Abraham], that he will command his children and his household after him, and they shall keep the way of the Lord, to do justice and judgment" (Genesis 18:19). Abraham trusted God and God trusted Abraham.

Faith is the kind of confidence in God that is based on experience. Faith is friendship with God, like that experienced by Abraham (who "was called the Friend of God"—James 2:23) or Moses, whom the Lord spoke with "face to face, as a man speaketh unto his friend" (Exodus 33:11).

Faith is exemplified by the Book of Mormon prophet Nephi, who with unwearyingness sought God's will and would not ask for anything contrary to it (see Helaman 10). We are maturing in faith when the same can be said of us.

Faith is not blind, wishful thinking. It is not unquestioning belief. Faith is not imposed upon us by birth, parentage, or culture. God does not compel us to have faith. All people are equally able to have faith, because all people are equally able to choose what they will believe or desire to believe. Those who desire something better in this life can give place for the word of God in their hearts.

The four friends of the man with palsy who lowered his bed through the roof chose to believe what they had heard about Jesus—that He was a healer. The sick man chose to believe what Jesus offered him, which was forgiveness of sin. They acted upon their beliefs by overcoming the obstacles that stood between them and the Savior. By doing so they entered into an experiment upon Christ's word. They reached out to have a relationship of love with God. This was the faith Christ saw in them.

If you join the man with palsy in seeking the light of the gospel, the good word of Christ, for your life, be prepared to have your perspective about life change. Said Alma: "O then, is not this real? I say unto you, Yea, because it is light; and whatsoever is light, is good, because it is discernible" (Alma 32:35). An experiment on God's word always brings discerning power with it. Often, the first thing a new believer can discern is how much he or she owes to God. As King Benjamin said: "If you should render all the thanks and praise which your whole soul has power to possess, to that God who has created you . . . yet ye would be unprofitable servants" (Mosiah 2:20–21).

By giving thanks, the desire to believe matures into a desire to please, just as occurred with King Benjamin's people, who said, "We are willing to enter into a covenant with God to do his will, and to be obedient to his commandments" (Mosiah 5:5). Believers desire to please God because they desire to know God, as pointed out by King Benjamin: "For how knoweth a man the master whom he has not served, and who is a stranger unto him, and is far from the thoughts and intents of his heart?" (Mosiah 5:13). Those who begin to know God learn to trust Him because, as King David wrote, "They that know thy name will put their trust in thee: for thou, Lord, hast not forsaken them that seek thee" (Psalm 9:10).

Trust in God, which is another name for faith, makes us strong in adversity, as Nephi proclaims:

> O wretched man that I am! Yea, my heart sorroweth because of my flesh; my soul grieveth because of mine iniquities.
>
> I am encompassed about, because of the temptations and the sins which do so easily beset me.
>
> And when I desire to rejoice, my heart groaneth because of my sins: nevertheless, I know in whom I have trusted.
>
> My God hath been my support; he hath led me through mine afflictions in the wilderness; and he hath preserved me upon the waters of the great deep.
>
> He hath filled me with his love." (2 Nephi 4:17–21)

Here, for me, is the heart of faith. Like Nephi, I know what a wretched man I am. With him, my soul grieves because of iniquity. And I am easily beset with temptations and sin. I have the choice whether I accept these problems as the limitations of my nature, or whether I believe the word of God, the gospel, which tells me I can repent and become something better than what I have been. If I choose to believe that people are prisoners of biology—driven by hormones or neurons or genes to behave according to unconquerable appetites—then I accept my fate as predetermined by nature's chaos. If I believe that, then the only meaning of freedom is that I am free from all responsibility but not free from misery. I choose instead what Nephi chooses: "I know in whom I have trusted."

I don't have the intimate kind of friendship with God that Nephi, Moses, and Abraham enjoyed. Unlike Nephi, I still ask amiss because I have not completely aligned my life with God's will. But I have perceived the beginnings of a love of God in my heart. This relationship with God that I call faith is a product of my efforts to experiment on God's word. It is not wishful thinking; it is discernible, it enlightens my understanding, and it is real. And it is a reality available to all men and women.

"The truth of God will go forth boldly, nobly, and independent," Joseph declared, "till it has penetrated every continent, visited every clime, swept every country, and sounded in every ear, till the purposes of God shall be accomplished, and the Great Jehovah shall say the work is done" (quoted in "The Wentworth Letter," *Ensign*, July 2002). This is the greatest movement ever begun in the history of the world. God reserves a special portion of his Spirit for those who join the movement and go forward with faith.

HOPE
HOW WE COME TO OURSELVES

I remember finding out when I was young that the mother of one of my friends had been involved in an auto-pedestrian accident. She had been driving her car down a neighborhood street, complying with all relevant traffic laws, when a child ran into the street in front of her and was killed on impact with her vehicle. Needless to say, she was devastated. She reworked the memory over and over, searching her soul and castigating herself for causing this child's death. She felt emotionally ruined. Her friends repeatedly tried to reassure her that she was not at fault and should not hold herself responsible, but no amount of reassurance could change what for her was the ultimate reality: if she had not been driving a car down that road at that moment, the child would still be living.

I remembered that woman years later while I was working as a resident physician in the emergency room at Primary Children's Medical Center in Salt Lake City, Utah. A child had been playing in piles of leaves on the street after dark. While in a leaf pile, the child was run over by a car. Probably unaware of the child in the pile of leaves, the driver had not stopped after hitting him. Rushed by ambulance to the emergency room, the child died there of massive injuries.

The incident was reported on the ten o'clock news that night, with a plea for any driver on that street during that particular evening to get in touch with the police. Imagine discovering the evidence of that fatal accident on your car the next morning. What would that discovery cost you? Peace of mind? Self-esteem?

Perhaps the ultimate sense of loss is experienced by the parent whose child dies. I had a family in my general practice in Reno, Nevada, with a newborn child. As it happened one night, the mother fell asleep nursing the baby in bed. When she awoke, the baby was dead—a SIDS death. After the funeral, the mother came into our clinic for a checkup, and we spent a long time talking. She was grieving and worrying that she had inadvertently caused the baby's death by suffocating the baby in her sleep. She felt emotionally lost. She felt worthless as a mother. She could not imagine how to recover.

We live in a mortal world, a world where even our best efforts may not be good enough. Our actions, though innocent or well intended, may have disastrous consequences for someone else. And then there are the times when we give less than our best—when we let prejudices, appetites, or laziness rule our behavior. We sin—and in addition to the spiritual harm we do to ourselves, others' lives are damaged. How much worse would be the personal feelings of my friend's mother if she had been late for a hair appointment and was speeding when she hit the child in the street?

A New Testament story relates to this:

> And the scribes and Pharisees brought unto him a woman taken in adultery; and when they had set her in the midst,
>
> They say unto him, Master, this woman was taken in adultery, in the very act.
>
> Now Moses in the law commanded us, that such should be stoned: but what sayest thou?
>
> This they said, tempting him, that they might have to accuse him. (John 8:3–6)

The adulterous woman's feelings must have been a mixture of fear for her life, shame for her mistakes, and perhaps horror for the situation she had inadvertently created—a situation that put Jesus at risk. For if He advocated for Mosaic law and agreed to her stoning, He would be in violation of Roman law and could be punished. If He did not advocate for the Mosaic punishment of stoning, He would be discredited as a teacher of God's law.

How many times do we put other people's ambitions, dreams, and purposes at risk by our selfishness? Many people find little solace in their own lives. Perhaps they have not suffered the death of a child and worried that they may have caused it, but they have had failures in personal relationships and the cumulative impact of those losses causes great mourning. These people have lost faith in themselves, have lost their confidence. They believe in Jesus but find it hard to believe in themselves. They wish to give of themselves but do not think they have anything to offer.

I believe that Jesus was talking about personal losses like these when He spoke the following parables:

> What man of you, having an hundred sheep, if he lose one of them, doth not leave the ninety and nine in the wilderness, and go after that which is lost, until he find it?
>
> And when he hath found it, he layeth it on his shoulder, rejoicing.
>
> And when he cometh home, he calleth together his friends and neighbours, saying unto them, Rejoice with me; for I have found my sheep which was lost.
>
> I say unto you, that likewise joy shall be in heaven over one sinner that repenteth, more than over ninety and nine just persons, which need no repentance.
>
> Either what woman having ten pieces of silver, if she lose one piece, doth not light a candle, and sweep the house, and seek diligently till she find it?
>
> And when she hath found it, she calleth her friends and her neighbours together, saying, Rejoice with me; for I have found the piece which I had lost.
>
> Likewise, I say unto you, there is joy in the presence of the angels of God over one sinner that repenteth. (Luke 15:4–10)

These are not parables about how to care for sheep or run a household. A shepherd does not leave ninety-nine sheep in the wilderness while looking for a single lost lamb. Nor does a householder have a neighborhood party after spending a day in search of a sum of money equal to a day's pay.

These are parables about how to restore lost peace of mind or lost confidence. Jesus is teaching us how God rejoices when you find that which is valuable within you.

Having the proper perspective about yourself is an essential part of Christian living. We are warned repeatedly about too much self-confidence, pride, or trusting in the arm of flesh. Overinflated egos place faith in themselves, not God, and have little use for other people. Thus, a proper understanding of oneself is essential to success in spirituality, because you cannot love God or your fellowmen if you love yourself too much. But an underinflated sense of self-worth is equally devastating to your spiritual nature. How can you have faith in a loving God if you do not consider yourself to be worthy of love? How can you act charitably to others if you have an uncharitable view of yourself?

The Apostle Paul wrote, "And now abideth faith, hope, charity, these three" (1 Corinthians 13:13). And the fourth section of the Doctrine and Covenants states that faith, hope, and charity are essential qualifications for the worker in the kingdom of God. Many scriptural references can be cited to the same effect—faith, hope, and charity are quintessential Christian virtues. We easily recognize faith and charity in the two great commandments as stated by Christ: "Thou shalt love the Lord thy God with all thy heart, and with all thy soul, and with all thy mind. This is the first and great commandment. And the second is like unto it, Thou shalt love thy neighbour as thyself. On these two commandments hang all the law and the prophets" (Matthew 22:37–40).

Faith is a loving relationship with God, and charity is love of our fellowmen. But we are not qualified for God's work until we also have hope. What relationship is characterized by the Christian principle of hope?

In answer to this question, Moroni quotes the ancient prophet Ether: "Wherefore, whoso believeth in God might with surety hope for a better world, yea, even a place at the right hand of God, which hope cometh of faith, maketh an anchor to the souls of men, which would make them sure and steadfast, always abounding in good works, being led to glorify God" (Ether 12:4). To paraphrase, faith in God changes something within the soul that makes us more sure of ourselves.

That quality born of faith within us that gives us an anchor for our souls, a different perspective about ourselves, is hope. So faith describes our relationship with God, and charity describes our relationship with other people, but hope is what we should think of ourselves. Hope is what my friend's mother needed after she saw a child die after being hit by her car. Hope is what my patient needed after the SIDS death of her baby.

Hope is what motivated the prodigal son to return to his father. You remember that the prodigal son took his inheritance and wasted it on riotous living:

> And when he had spent all, there arose a mighty famine in that land; and he began to be in want.
>
> And he went and joined himself to a citizen of that country; and he sent him into his fields to feed swine.
>
> And he would fain have filled his belly with the husks that the swine did eat: and no man gave unto him.
>
> And when he came to himself, he said, How many hired servants of my father's have bread enough and to spare, and I perish with hunger!
>
> I will arise and go to my father. (Luke 15:14–18)

Why did he decide to return to his father? Because he "came to himself"; he realized who he really was. He rejected the image of himself held previously when he had money to spend and people who flattered him. Hope, the true image of our nature, does not come about because of externalities like money or the praise of men. He also rejected the image of himself as worthy only to live like a pig, dying in misery because of past mistakes. If we allow a poor self-image to paralyze our spirit, we are not living by faith but by the doubts that haunt us in this uncertain, mortal world.

Christ Himself is the key to a proper perspective about self. When He talked of leaving the ninety-nine to find the one, He was promising to be in search of each of us at the moment we need His influence. And He did not merely talk about giving each of us hope—He lived the principle. When the woman taken in adultery was brought before Him, he did not think first of the danger to Himself inherent in the situation. His focus was on the woman.

Rather than withdraw from the situation, he sized up his audience and stated, "He that is without sin among you, let him first cast a stone at her" (John 8:7). And when left alone with the woman, Jesus said, "Neither do I condemn thee: go, and sin no more" (John 8:11). When we likewise are alone among our accusers, even if we are doing the accusing to ourselves, Christ will be there—not condemning, but encouraging us to live a better life.

Moses understood the need for hope in one's life better than did most ancient prophets. Raised in the royal house, he nonetheless had developed a sense of charity that made him unable to tolerate the injustice of slavery. And he had the faith to turn aside and see the burning bush. But when called to lead the children of Israel out of Egypt, his sense of self failed, and he pleaded, "Who am I, that I should go unto Pharaoh, and that I should bring forth the children of Israel out of Egypt?" (Exodus 3:11). But after a lifetime of service to God, under extraordinarily trying circumstances, Moses offered the following:

> For this commandment which I command thee this day, it is not hidden from thee, neither is it far off.
>
> It is not in heaven, that thou shouldest say, Who shall go up for us to heaven, and bring it unto us, that we may hear it, and do it?
>
> Neither is it beyond the sea, that thou shouldest say, Who shall go over the sea for us, and bring it unto us, that we may hear it, and do it?
>
> But the word is very nigh unto thee, in thy mouth, and in thy heart, that thou mayest do it. (Deuteronomy 30:11–14)

Moses, who feared failure and held no hope for his own success, had learned that it is in our human nature to succeed spiritually. Relying on God with faith and seeking to bless the lives of others with acts of charity both require that we have hope for ourselves, hope that we can accomplish what God asks us to do.

Moroni saw his family, friends, and civilization lost through violent carnage and found himself alone in a world that wanted him dead—nonetheless, he knew and lived the principle of hope. He quoted his father, Mormon:

And again, my beloved brethren, I would speak unto you concerning hope. How is it that ye can attain faith, save ye shall have hope?

And what is it that ye shall hope for? Behold I say unto you that ye shall have hope through the atonement of Christ and the power of his resurrection, to be raised unto life eternal, and this because of your faith in him according to the promise.

Wherefore, if a man have faith he must needs have hope; for without faith there cannot be any hope. . . .

Wherefore, my beloved brethren, pray unto the Father with all the energy of heart, that ye may be filled with this love, which he hath bestowed upon all who are true followers of his Son, Jesus Christ; that ye may become the sons of God; that when he shall appear we shall be like him, for we shall see him as he is; that we may have this hope; that we may be purified even as he is pure. Amen. (Moroni 7:40–42, 48)

Hope is a concept of ourselves that accepts our mortal state as a time when we need the help of Jesus, who, through the Atonement, can save us from our weaknesses and raise us up to a state of purity, even as He is pure. Hope avoids the error of pride, in which we think of ourselves as too self-sufficient to need any help from God or anyone.

But hope also avoids the error of despair, in which we are more impressed by our failings than we are with the Savior's ability to help us. Hopelessness is actually a statement of unbelief, because in it we give Christ no credit for His hard-earned power to bring to pass our personal salvation. Remember Alma's words to the righteous and enlightened people of the city of Gideon:

And he shall go forth, suffering pains and afflictions and temptations of every kind; and this that the word might be fulfilled which saith he will take upon him the pains and the sicknesses of his people.

And he will take upon him death, that he may loose the bands of death which bind his people; and he will take upon him their infirmities, that his bowels may be filled with mercy, according to the flesh, that he may know according to the flesh how to succor his people according to their infirmities.

Now the Spirit knoweth all things; nevertheless the Son of God suffereth according to the flesh that he might take upon him the sins of his people, that he might blot out their transgressions according to the power of his deliverance; and now behold, this is the testimony which is in me.

Now I say unto you that ye must repent. . . .

Yea, I say unto you come and fear not, and lay aside every sin, which easily doth beset you, which doth bind you down to destruction, yea, come and go forth, and show unto God that ye are willing to repent of your sins. . . .

And whosoever doeth this . . . he shall have eternal life." (Alma 7:11–16)

Ultimately, if we are to have hope, we must practice repentance before God. Those who are too proud to admit that they have done wrong cannot have hope, because they cannot repent. Those who are too despairing to admit that they can repent and become better people cannot have hope either and ultimately do not have faith, no matter what they pray or say they believe.

Before he ever received and read the Book of Mormon, Joseph Smith had the insight to follow Moroni's suggested pathway to hope. His own history records the following:

During the space of time which intervened between the time I had the vision and the year eighteen hundred and twenty-three— having been forbidden to join any of the religious sects of the day, and being of very tender years, and persecuted by those who ought to have been my friends and to have treated me kindly, and if they supposed me to be deluded to have endeavored in a proper and affectionate manner to have reclaimed me—I was left to all kinds of temptations; and, mingling with all kinds of society, I frequently fell into many foolish errors, and displayed the weakness of youth, and the foibles of human nature; which, I am sorry to say, led me into divers temptations, offensive in the sight of God. In making this confession, no one need suppose me guilty of any great or malignant sins. A disposition to commit such was never in my nature. But I was guilty of levity, and sometimes associated with jovial company, etc., not consistent with that character which ought to be maintained by one who was called of God as I had been. But this will not seem very strange to any one who recollects my youth, and is acquainted with my native cheery temperament.

In consequence of these things, I often felt condemned for my weakness and imperfections; when, on the evening of the above-mentioned twenty-first of September, after I had retired to my bed for the night, I betook myself to prayer and supplication to Almighty God for forgiveness of all my sins and follies, and also for a manifestation to me, that I might know of my state and standing before him; for I had full confidence in obtaining a divine manifestation, as I previously had one. (Joseph Smith—History 1:28–29)

Which of us has not committed many foolish errors and displayed weaknesses and the foibles of human nature? Which of us has not succumbed to temptations offensive in the sight of God? Which of us has not acted in a manner inconsistent with the character of one called by God? In these faults, I am as guilty as Joseph claims to be, for I share in the common tendencies of humanity. I have been insensitive to others, held prejudices and grudges, and laughed at others' weaknesses. I have been vain and vulgar. And in my more serious moments, I have pondered on these failings and wondered about how many times I have hurt someone's feelings or failed to render to someone the aid and comfort needed. When one of my patients committed suicide many years ago, I felt despair for myself because I thought perhaps I could have done something differently for that man.

Joseph Smith, too, had cause to despair because of his personal weakness. When he handed the Book of Mormon manuscript over to Martin Harris, he did so despite God's strict and repeated instructions not to do so. When he discovered that the manuscript was lost, he received the revelation now known as the third section of the Doctrine and Covenants, which says: "For although a man may have many revelations, and have power to do many mighty works, yet if he boasts in his own strength, and sets at naught the counsels of God, and follows after the dictates of his own will and carnal desires, he must fall and incur the vengeance of a just God upon him" (D&C 3:4).

Note that the Lord reprimands Joseph for not having the proper perspective about himself. In other words, Joseph was not living according to the Christian principle of hope—he thought he had already become spiritually self-sufficient and knew what was best, despite God's counsel. But lest Joseph make the equally grievous error of despair, God counsels further: "But remember, God is merciful; therefore, repent of that which thou hast done which is contrary to the commandment which I gave you, and thou art still chosen, and art again called to the work" (D&C 3:10). In this case, repentance took months. But the lesson was well learned. Joseph did not make the error of being prideful again.

In the jail at Liberty, however, Joseph Smith did suffer despair, the other threat to hope. He had been months in chains over a bitterly cold winter while the Saints were suffering exposure and hunger, and he prayed: "O God, where art thou? . . . Let thine anger be kindled against our enemies; and, in the fury of thine heart, with thy sword avenge us of our wrongs. Remember thy suffering saints, O our God" (D&C 121:1, 5–6). God's answer was not one of fury but a reminder of faith, hope, and charity: "Let thy bowels also be full of charity towards all men, and to the household of faith, and let virtue garnish thy thoughts unceasingly; then shall thy confidence wax strong in the presence of God; and the doctrine of the priesthood shall distil upon thy soul as the dews from heaven" (D&C 121:45).

Hope is having confidence in the presence of God; Joseph learned that hope is not dependent on anything outside of our soul. Hope is not dependent on things being fair in this life. It was not fair that my friend's mother killed the child with her car, nor was it fair that my patient's baby died. The extermination order issued by the governor of Missouri against the Mormons was not fair either, and Joseph was unfairly imprisoned for months. It was not fair to the prodigal son that his friends abandoned him in his hour of need. But the solution to unfairness is not found in self-pity, despair, or seeking some kind of external compensation. The solution is to come to yourself, like the prodigal son, and find the value of your own soul. Recognize, as did Moses, that the power to obey God's commands is already in your heart. Repent, as did Joseph Smith, and pray with the energy of your heart while having charity toward all men. Have faith in Christ, Alma taught, and you will have hope that you can be purified as He is pure.

If we fail at having hope by clinging to pride or despair, we cannot repent. And as King Benjamin said: "Therefore if that man repenteth not, and remaineth and dieth an enemy to God, the demands of divine justice do awaken his immortal soul to a lively sense of his own guilt, which doth cause him to shrink from the presence of the Lord, and doth fill his breast with guilt, and pain, and anguish, which is like an unquenchable fire, whose flame ascendeth up forever and ever" (Mosiah 2:38).

When our moment of truth comes at the judgment bar of Christ, we will either have given in to pride or to despair and will have failed to repent. In that case, we will have no confidence before Christ, and we will choose to leave His presence because our lively sense of guilt will make us uncomfortable near Him. Or we will have lived lives of hope and have earned confidence before God and a desire to be with Him.

CHARITY
THE PURE LOVE OF CHRIST

There were two occasions when Jesus made a whip with which He cleared the temple court in Jerusalem. I imagine He must have acted with great zeal, energy, and fury on those occasions. He would have had to shout while applying His whip and overthrowing the tables.

I have often wondered how the violence of this act could be considered loving. How can the same person use a whip and also teach the principle of charity by saying: "Love your enemies, bless them that curse you, do good to them that hate you, and pray for them which despitefully use you, and persecute you; that ye may be the children of your Father which is in heaven: for he maketh his sun to rise on the evil and on the good, and sendeth rain on the just and on the unjust" (Matthew 5:44–45). Because Christ is our example of love, we must be able to find the love of God in these episodes.

Generally, when people act with great zeal and fury toward their fellowman, they are not expressing love. On Grosvenor Square across from the US embassy in London, there is a small memorial to the UK citizens who lost their lives on September 11, 2001, in New York's World Trade Center. The inscription across the top of the monument reads: "Grief is the price we pay for love." That sentiment reminds me of a verse in the Doctrine and Covenants: "Thou shalt live together in love, insomuch that thou shalt weep for the loss of them that die" (D&C 42:45).

For most of us, tears flow naturally when someone we love passes on. However, scripture reveals that a characteristic of our time will be the number of unloved and unloving people who pass through this life without mourning for or being mourned by anyone. Speaking to his Apostles just before the Crucifixion and explaining to them what conditions will prevail upon the earth before His Second Coming, Christ said: "Then shall many be offended, and shall betray one another, and shall hate one another. . . . And because iniquity shall abound, the love of many shall wax cold" (Matthew 24:10–12).

The same conditions existed before the Flood: "And the children of men were numerous upon all the face of the land. And in those days Satan had great dominion among men, and raged in their hearts; and from thenceforth came wars and bloodshed; and a man's hand was against his own brother, in administering death, because of secret works, seeking for power" (Moses 6:15).

Of our day, Joseph Smith prophesied: "And in that day shall be heard of wars and rumors of wars, and the whole earth shall be in commotion, and men's hearts shall fail them, . . . and the love of men shall wax cold, and iniquity shall abound" (D&C 45:26–27). In a separate verse, he added, "for fear shall come upon all people" (D&C 88:91).

It seems to me that Jesus was thinking of the chilling effect of fear on love when He told the parable of the good Samaritan (see Luke 10:30–37). The priest and the Levite passed by their wounded fellow Jew "on the other side." They feared getting involved, perhaps because of the robbers, or lack of time, or the messiness of the situation, or the cost, or maybe they thought he was going to die anyway. The Samaritan very likely had all the same fears—but added to those was the very real likely fear that his nationality would be unacceptable to a fastidious Jew.

In that well-known parable, Jesus taught us to push past our fears and reach out to our neighbors, by which He clearly meant everyone. John, the beloved Apostle, said: "There is no fear in love; but perfect love casteth out fear: because fear hath torment. He that feareth is not made perfect in love. We love him, because he first loved us. If a man say, I love God, and hateth his brother, he is a liar: for he that loveth not his brother whom he hath seen, how can he love God whom he hath not seen?" (1 John 4:18–20).

Faith, which is love of God, is the first principle of the gospel and is founded on the preeminent love God has for us. But the second commandment, to love God's children, is the practical expression of faith: we cannot expect to have a meaningful relationship with God if we through fear let our love of men wax cold. Said Jesus at His final Passover: "He that hath my commandments, and keepeth them, he it is that loveth me. . . . If a man love me, he will keep my words" (John 14:21, 23). "If ye keep my commandments, ye shall abide in my love" (John 15:10).

At that same Passover meal, while walking to the Garden of Gethsemane to begin the ultimate act of love, Jesus stated and restated: "A new commandment I give unto you, that ye love one another; as I have loved you, that ye also love one another. By this shall all men know that ye are my disciples, if ye have love one to another" (John 13:34–35).

Recorded just a few chapters later in the Gospel of John, Jesus said, "This is my commandment, that ye love one another, as I have loved you. Greater love hath no man than this, that a man lay down his life for his friends. . . . These things I command you, that ye love one another" (John 15: 12–13, 17).

Jesus began this final teaching by washing the feet of His disciples, saying: "If I then, your Lord and Master, have washed your feet; ye also ought to wash one another's feet. For I have given you an example, that ye should do as I have done to you" (John 13:14–15). And Jesus ended this teaching by praying for His friends, saying: "And I have declared unto them thy name, and will declare it: that the love wherewith thou has loved me may be in them, and I in them" (John 17:26). As we overcome our fears and serve each other, we serve God, and we become the answer to Christ's prayer.

Of this love, Nephi wrote, "The Lord God hath given a commandment that all men should have charity, which charity is love" (2 Nephi 26:30). In the Book of Mormon, Moroni further explained, "Charity is the pure love of Christ" (Moroni 7:47). Paul tells us to "follow after charity" (1 Corinthians 14:1), which he specifically differentiates from donating money: "And though I bestow all my goods to feed the poor . . . and have not charity, it profiteth me nothing" (1 Corinthians 13:3).

We probably will not weep over those for whom we have merely donated money. Charity requires more than that. Charity is the quintessential Christian virtue—the savor with which we should salt the earth (see Matthew 5:13) and the light of the candle that should so shine to glorify God (see Matthew 5:16). Without charity, your heart will fail you and wax cold, and you will join the masses of modern men whose fears keep them from living together in love. Because each personal relationship is a risk they are unwilling to take, the only personal relationships these unloving and unloved modern people can cultivate are based on intense personal control, offense, betrayal, or hatred with intent to maximize personal power. This is the zero sum game of modern materialism, where every success by someone else is alleged to subtract from what I can get for myself.

These unloved and unloving people so characteristic of human society in the fullness of times are like the people on earth before the Flood, about whom God said to Enoch: "Behold these thy brethren; they are the workmanship of mine own hands, and I gave unto them their knowledge, in the day I created them; and in the Garden of Eden, gave I unto man his agency; and unto thy brethren have I said, and also given commandment, that they should love one another, and that they should choose me, their Father; but behold, they are without affection, and they hate their own blood" (Moses 7:32–33).We are these people, and we are in a torment of our own making when we do not have the courage to risk accommodating the unique needs of our neighbors. God weeps for us, and Jesus suffered for our sins, but we know only hypocrisy and misery if we cannot learn how to love with the vigor that Christ loves. Charity is the only power with a chance to break through this cycle of suffering, keep us safe from it, and allow us to draw others out of it.

After the heartbreak of the Crucifixion, during which Peter allowed his fears to chill his heart into betrayal of the Savior, and despite the exhilaration of the Resurrection, when left to his agency, Peter went back to fishing and took six other Apostles with him (see John 21). They spent a fruitless night fishing, only to have a man shout instructions from shore at sunrise that they should be fishing from the other side of the boat. Upon doing so, they immediately caught more than they could handle. John, the author of the account, claims the initial insight that their shore-based benefactor must be Jesus.

Peter swam the one hundred yards to shore, the sooner to greet the Savior. There, he was stung by Jesus asking three times: "Simon, son of Jonas, lovest thou me?" Peter answered three times with the insistent "Thou knowest that I love thee." Jesus did not contradict but said only, "Feed my sheep."

Charity is not an intellectual exercise, nor is it an emotion. We cannot feel charity, and it cannot be a thought experiment. You cannot store up charity or borrow it from someone else. You cannot fall in love or have a charitable relationship without effort, because you must apply yourself constantly to create love. Peter felt that he loved Christ, and he intellectually knew Jesus was resurrected, but he could not truly love the Savior unless he worked at it as he had formerly worked at fishing.

Charity is something we do, a principle by which we live, and it is the actual expression of faith, our love for God. If we fail to have charity, we fail to be like Jesus or to know who He is. It is the highest of standards. It is found at the end of the Sermon on the Mount, the greatest discourse on charity ever given:

> Not every one that saith unto me, Lord, Lord, shall enter into the kingdom of Heaven; but he that doeth the will of my Father which is in heaven.
>
> Many will say to me in that day, Lord, Lord, have we not prophesied in thy name? and in thy name have cast out devils? And in thy name done many wonderful works?
>
> And then will I profess unto them, I never knew you: depart from me, ye that work iniquity. (Matthew 7:21–23)

Nothing can take the place of charity. Charity is how the world can recognize a Christian; charity is how to be a Christian; charity is the only means available to teach Christianity.

Like Peter, we must each make a choice between Christ and our worldly pursuits. Success in worldly pursuits, even on the scale described in this story, with nets sagging with fish, must be considered in light of Christ's question to Peter: "Simon, son of Jonas, lovest thou me more than these" fish? And like Peter, we cannot get by with mere words of reassurance, "Yea, Lord; thou knowest I love thee." For He has said, "He that hath my commandments, and keepeth them, he it is that loveth me." And this is His commandment: that we love one another as He loved us.

This is not to say that if fishing is our livelihood, we must give it up in the pursuit of charity—instead, we must find a way to both fish and live life with charity. It is not money but "the love of money [that] is the root of all evil" (1 Timothy 6:10), a flaw found equally among both the wealthy and the poor. Said Jesus: "Lay not up for yourselves treasures upon earth, where moth and rust doth corrupt, and where thieves break through and steal: But lay up for yourselves treasures in heaven, where neither moth nor rust doth corrupt, and where thieves do not break through nor steal: For where your treasure is, there will your heart be also" (Matthew 6:19–21). How and what we love determines our eternal inventory. The scriptures teach us whom to love and how to love them.

Beginning with birth, our first experiences in mortality should be shaped by family, a learning laboratory for love. Within that intimate circle, parents have a special obligation to teach their children "to love one another, and to serve one another" (Mosiah 4:15). Children are to honor fathers and mothers (see Exodus 20:12). Husbands should love their wives "as Christ also loved the church, and gave himself for it" (Ephesians 5:25), while the desire of the wife shall be to her husband (see Genesis 3:16). Brothers and sisters are to be each other's keepers (see Genesis 4:9). Each of us is commanded to join a family circle with the steadfastness of Ruth, who sets the biblical standard for love and service within extended families; she "clave" unto Naomi, her mother-in-law, saying, "Intreat me not to leave thee, or to return from following after thee: for whither thou goest, I will go; and where thou lodgest, I will lodge: thy people shall be my people, and thy God my God" (Ruth 1:16).

Each of us begins this life in need of love and nurture. Later in life, our nearness to God will be determined by how loving we have been toward family members. As Nephi's brother Jacob bluntly chastised the Nephites for breaking the hearts of their wives and children, he used the Lamanites as an example of how family life should be: "Behold, their husbands love their wives, and their wives love their husbands; and their husbands and their wives love their children" (Jacob 3:7). Because the Lamanites loved better within families, Jacob pointed out that the Nephites were less righteous even though they possessed truer doctrine.

Being endowed with correct gospel principles offers us no protection if we violate the sacred trust of love within our family circle. So many unloved and unloving modern people fail to have charity because they fail in their families. Parents who walk away from their opportunity to love their children often do so because they do not know or do not care what Paul teaches about charity: "Charity suffereth long, and is kind; charity envieth not; charity vaunteth not itself, is not puffed up, doth not behave itself unseemly, seeketh not her own, is not easily provoked, thinketh no evil; rejoiceth not in iniquity, but rejoiceth in the truth; beareth all things, believeth all things, hopeth all things, endureth all things" (1 Corinthians 13:4–7).

In the family, the needs of others must always supersede our own. Each of us must learn to not behave unseemly, seek not our own, not be provoked, and to endure all things. Children learn to do those things if they are shown how by older relatives. Adults who are long-suffering and kind with children, who seek first to care for the child and are not puffed up in their own concerns, will earn a privileged and intimate acquaintance with their younger family members. They will have front-row seats for watching the miraculous transition from infancy to maturity; they will be a trusted and beloved friend throughout the child's life. These blessings, if we are worthy, are the gift of a loving God to each of us through the institution of the family. How completely mistaken are the people I have seen who decide that caring for a child is boring, is too taxing, or is interfering with their own personal pursuits—and who walk away from their family circle seeking self-fulfillment through divorce or abandonment.

Joseph Smith taught us to think broadly about the definition of family. Elijah the prophet has come, as foreseen by Malachi, to "turn the heart of the fathers to the children, and the heart of the children to their fathers" (Malachi 4:6). This phrase, alone among all verses of scripture, is found in all four books of scriptural canon in the Church, though in modern scripture it is rendered as quoted by Moroni: "And he shall plant in the hearts of the children the promises made to the fathers, and the hearts of the children shall turn to their fathers" (D&C 2; Joseph Smith—History 1:39). Joseph F. Smith, former president of the Church and nephew of Joseph Smith, taught that these words "[foreshadow] the great work to be done in the temples of the Lord in the dispensation of the fulness of times, for the redemption of the dead, and the sealing of the children to their parents" so that all people who have ever lived on this earth can "be partakers of all blessings which were held in reserve for them that love" God (D&C 138:48, 52). Through redemption of the dead, we are blessed to be able to tangibly love all generations of our family.

But the Savior did not restrict our obligation to love to bloodlines. In His exemplary prayer, He said: "Thy kingdom come" (Matthew 6:10), meaning that Christ desired the kingdom of God to come to earth. To that end, Christ Himself has in every dispensation established a church, an organization of His believers, who associate with each other to bring to pass as a group what individuals cannot achieve working alone. Just as we do now, the people in Jesus's time delayed the hard work of perfecting the Saints but loved to speculate about the coming of God's kingdom on earth: "And when he was demanded of the Pharisees, when the kingdom of God should come, he answered them and said, The kingdom of God cometh not with observation: Neither shall they say, Lo here! or, lo there! for, behold, the kingdom of God is within you" (Luke 17:20–21). In other words, you cannot be an independent observer of the arrival of the kingdom of God because it can only be established by you in your own heart.

Membership in the kingdom of God on earth is based on a desire to have charity, as Alma taught:

As ye are desirous to come into the fold of God, and to be called his people, and are willing to bear one another's burdens, that they may be light;

Yea, and are willing to mourn with those that mourn; yea, and comfort those that stand in need of comfort . . .

Now I say unto you, if this be the desire of your hearts, what have you against being baptized in the name of the Lord, as a witness before him that ye have entered into a covenant with him, that ye will serve him and keep his commandments? (Mosiah 18:8–10)

The kingdom of God cannot come without people practicing love one for another. It is no use talking about the Second Coming if we do not have charity.

During the early years of my marriage, our oldest child fell very ill while I was away from home and unreachable by phone. My wife needed someone to help her bear that burden; she stood in need of comfort. Since she could not reach me, and since she did not have immediate family nearby, she called her mother, who lived seven hundred miles away. Her mother told her to call her home teacher. My wife couldn't do that because, although we had been in the ward for two years, we did not know who was assigned to visit us—simply because they never had visited us.

Our son eventually received a priesthood blessing, but that home teacher failed his opportunity to build the kingdom of God on earth. He lost his chance to fulfill the covenant of the Book of Mormon. Said Ezra Taft Benson, "[Home teaching] is the heart of caring, of loving, of reaching out to the one—both the active and the less active. It is priesthood compassionate service. It is how we express our faith in practical works. It is one of the tests of true discipleship. It is the heart of the activation effort of the Church" ("To the Home Teachers of the Church," *Ensign*, May 1987). This applies, of course, to both men and women in the Church's current ministering program.

I remember many of the people I have come to know through home teaching. During my years in medical school and residency, each month,

I visited a young couple with three children. They showed little interest in joining with me and my family at church meetings. He worked in the cement business and had to travel a hundred miles each way to work. I also visited a young unmarried mother with an infant who lived with two gay men. For a couple years I visited a retired air force colonel, his wife, and daughter. I also visited regularly with an elderly widower during the last decade of his life. As a young man, he emigrated from Germany to the United States. Though gradually fading, he was fiercely independent.

Some of my home teaching families have welcomed me. Others have been wary. Some never invited me into the house, though they were glad to get a call or a small gift at the door. But I never had a contact with my home teaching households without feeling a spiritual endorsement. Without home teaching, church attendance can become networking instead of fellowshipping. I try to remember that eternal life is based not on who you know, but on who you love and serve. All in the Church are called to minister, but those who fail to try are not chosen.

There is another way we can be called in the Church but not chosen, according to revelation by Joseph Smith, and that is by exercising unrighteous dominion, which we do "when we undertake to cover our sins, or to gratify our pride, our vain ambition, or to exercise control or dominion or compulsion upon the souls of the children of men" (D&C 121:37). If we cannot admit our shortcomings even to ourselves, we will not want other people to know about them either. We will have vain ambition to project a more competent, caring image of ourselves than is really the case.

To intentionally attempt to induce people to perceive us as something better than what we really are is manipulative. Manipulation is the essence of unrighteous dominion. This is our modern-day Rameumptom, where we stand and thank God that we are a chosen and holy people and then return to our homes and don't speak of God again (see Alma 31:18–23). Christ spake a parable about this:

> And he spake this parable unto certain which trusted in themselves that they were righteous, and despised others:

Two men went up into the temple to pray; the one a Pharisee, and the other a publican.

The Pharisee stood and prayed thus with himself, God, I thank thee, that I am not as other men are, extortioners, unjust, adulterers, or even as this publican.

I fast twice in the week, I give tithes of all that I possess.

And the publican, standing afar off, would not lift up so much as his eyes unto heaven, but smote upon his breast, saying, God be merciful to me a sinner.

I tell you, this man went down to his house justified rather than the other: for every one that exalteth himself shall be abased; and he that humbleth himself shall be exalted. (Luke 18:9–14)

When we exalt ourselves, the pride we gratify is actually a fear that someone will get close enough to us to discover the weaknesses we are trying to hide. We fear the person who is different from our manipulative norm, who forces us to stretch ourselves to accommodate his needs, because we might not succeed with him and thereby might reveal our weakness. When called to lead, we avoid asking our fellow servant for more effort, lest we reveal our own failings. We euphemize the situation rather than hold ourselves to an uncomfortable gospel standard.

These fears force us to live in hypocrisy, which pacifies us, cheats our souls, and leads us carefully down to hell (see 2 Nephi 28:21). The antidote for unrighteous dominion, with its consequent hypocrisy, is spelled out by Joseph Smith, who teaches that we must live "by persuasion, by long-suffering, by gentleness and meekness, and by love unfeigned; by kindness, and pure knowledge, which shall greatly enlarge the soul without hypocrisy, and without guile—reproving betimes with sharpness, when moved upon by the Holy Ghost; and then showing forth afterwards an increase of love toward him whom thou hast reproved" (D&C 121:41–43).

A direct and clear reproof, which is constructive criticism delivered with clarity, is one of the most loving things we can do for someone who is mistaken. To avoid an uncomfortable conflict is to pretend a problem does not exist, which is hypocrisy. Charity, which is nine parts ceaseless effort to love and support mixed with one part unflinching honesty, is the only antidote to unrighteous dominion. To do less is to fail to help others better themselves and to fail to establish the kingdom of God within us. This is our equivalent of taking a whip and clearing the temple court.

Inevitably, as we reprove with sharpness, offense may be given or taken. Christ provided instructions to us in these matters: "Therefore if thou bring thy gift to the altar, and there rememberest that thy brother hath ought against thee; leave there thy gift before the altar, and go thy way; first be reconciled to thy brother, and then come and offer thy gift" (Matthew 5:23–24).

The most poignant scriptural story of reconciliation is that of Joseph of Egypt with his brothers. Immediately upon receiving them as they seek to buy grain during a famine, Joseph recognizes his ten older brothers. He concocts a scheme on the spot to assure that his younger brother, Benjamin, is brought to Egypt. Because he is in a position of trust in Egypt, his loyalties are to Pharaoh. He yearns to reconcile with his family immediately but must be sure they are ready to repent of the injustice they imposed upon him.

Joseph weeps when he first hears them confess to each other how guilty they are for their nefarious act. Still, he must know that they have spiritually matured to the point that they would accept harm to themselves rather than cause another in the family to suffer. So Joseph retains Simeon in bondage, expecting the others to return from the land of Canaan with Benjamin. His first sight of his younger brother brings him to tears again. When Joseph threatens to keep Benjamin permanently, the true repentance of his brothers is manifest as Judah pleads to take Benjamin's place in bondage in order to spare their father any further grief. Joseph then knows his brothers are prepared to reconcile with him, and he reveals himself to them and says: "Now therefore be not grieved, nor angry with yourselves, that ye sold me hither: for God did send me before you to preserve life" (Genesis 45:5). He forgives them frankly and welcomes them back into his life; they in turn are grateful for another chance to live with Joseph in love.

Reconciliation is a bilateral process; both parties must work toward a trusting relationship, or no progress is possible. Forgiveness, on the other hand, is unilateral. That is why the Lord has commanded: "Wherefore, I say unto you, that ye ought to forgive one another; for he that forgiveth not his brother his trespasses standeth condemned before the Lord; for there remaineth in him the greater sin. I, the Lord, will forgive whom I will forgive, but of you it is required to forgive all men" (D&C 64:9–10). We all must be forgiven, and our opportunity to enjoy God's forgiveness depends on our willingness to forgive our fellowmen: "For if ye forgive men their trespasses, your heavenly Father will also forgive you: but if ye forgive not men their trespasses, neither will your Father forgive your trespasses" (Matthew 6:14–15). As the Savior said, the blessing of mercy is reserved for the merciful (see Matthew 5:7).

But we are not only to love our families and our fellow Saints. Once King Benjamin became persuaded that his people had "come to the knowledge of the glory of God" and had "tasted [God's] love," he instructed his people (in the second-best sermon on charity available in scripture):

> And now, . . . for the sake of retaining a remission of your sins from day to day, that ye may walk guiltless before God—I would that ye should impart of your substance to the poor, every man according to that which he hath, such as feeding the hungry, clothing the naked, visiting the sick and administering to their relief. . . .
>
> And see that all these things are done in wisdom and order; for it is not requisite that a man should run faster than he has strength." (Mosiah 4:26–27)

We cannot retain the effects of our baptismal covenant if we support an uncaring society. Where there is hunger, exposure, and untreated illness, there is dereliction in fulfilling our baptismal covenants. No one man alone has the strength to solve these pervasive societal problems, but as an entire society, with wise and orderly use of resources, we can fulfill these essential Christian obligations.

This was the last principle Jesus taught in public before His Crucifixion. In the parable of the sheep and goats, all nations are gathered before the Son of Man in His glory, and He separates them to the right and the left. Those on the right are beckoned into life eternal because their national priorities are right: they've cared for the needs of the hungry, thirsty, exposed, lonely, ill, and imprisoned. Those on the left go away to everlasting punishment because "inasmuch as ye did it not to one of the least of these, ye did it not to me" (see Matthew 25:31–46). It is not coincidental that the last thing Jesus taught on earth is presented as the first thing He will ask about in heaven. Each of us individually will bear personal responsibility for our part in the actions or inaction of the society we help to build.

Characteristically, the Old Testament prophets are more colorful about their discussion of this gospel principle because they saw firsthand the ultimate result of an uncaring society. Ezekiel described it this way:

> Son of man, prophesy against the shepherds of Israel, prophesy, and say unto them, Thus saith the Lord God unto the shepherds; Woe be to the shepherds of Israel that do feed themselves! should not the shepherds feed the flocks?
>
> Ye eat the fat, and ye clothe you with the wool, ye kill them that are fed: but ye feed not the flock.
>
> The diseased have ye not strengthened, neither have ye healed that which was sick, neither have ye bound up that which was broken, neither have ye brought again that which was driven away, neither have ye sought that which was lost; but with force and with cruelty have ye ruled them.
>
> And they were scattered, because there is no shepherd: and they became meat to all the beasts of the field, when they were scattered.
>
> My sheep wandered through all the mountains, and upon every high hill: yea, my flock was scattered upon all the face of the earth, and none did search or seek after them. (Ezekiel 34:2–6)

When we act with charity among our fellowmen, we proclaim the gospel. No one, not even our enemies, will fail to notice what is done with charity. In the Book of Mormon, when Ammon and his brothers left Zarahemla on their mission to preach the gospel to the Lamanites, they were laughed to scorn and told to take up arms and fight with rather than teach their enemies. But they chose charity: they were patient in suffering, visited in Lamanite homes, taught in the streets, entered the churches, and allowed themselves to be cast out, mocked, spit upon, slapped, stoned, bound, and imprisoned. In the end, their loving ministry caused a great Lamanite change of heart, which Ammon knew was sincere, "because of their love towards their brethren" (see Alma 26:27–33)—a love characterized as greater than any in all the land. As was demonstrated by Ammon, we cannot tell our neighbors about that love; we must personify it. Charity, along with hope and faith, qualifies us for missionary work (see D&C 4).

Pulitzer Prize winner Wallace Stegner, who spent his youth in Utah and later characterized himself as a non-Mormon but not a Mormon hater, wrote: "[The Mormon pioneers] were the most systematic, organized, disciplined, and successful pioneers in [American] history" (*The Gathering of Zion: The Story of the Mormon Trail* [Lincoln: University of Nebraska Press, 1996], 6). Faithful members of the Church are fond of that assessment; the quote is posted on the wall of the Church's visitors center in Winter Quarters, Nebraska.

In that same visitors center is a replica of the tiny cabins built by the vanguard Mormon pioneers for the winter of 1846–47. It is meant to impress us with the sacrifice of the Saints in that place. On my first visit there, however, I overheard a young woman say that she wished she had had such a nice house when she was growing up. She explained that she was born and raised in extreme poverty in Guatemala, with virtually no housing. She joined the Church with her family and had managed to immigrate to the United States. Her statement should remind us that while the pioneering done by the Latter-day Saints in the nineteenth century is now judged the best in history and allowed the kingdom of God on earth to be established, to our generation is given a different kingdom-building challenge.

We have a pioneering work of charity to do; we must build families and establish the kingdom of God worldwide. The mission of the Church is a mission of charity. President Gordon B. Hinckley powerfully reminded us of that mission:

> Whatever pertains to human welfare is the rightful concern of the Church. The prophets and seers of all ages have been champions of the poor and helpless. The Church cannot be less. So it has always cared for its needy. . . . A man out of work is of special moment to the Church because, deprived of his inheritance, he is on trial as Job was on trial—for his integrity. As days lengthen into weeks and months and even years of adversity, the hurt grows deeper, and he is sorely tempted to "curse God and die." Continued economic dependence breaks him; it humiliates him if he is strong, spoils him if he is weak. Sensitive or calloused, despondent or indifferent, rebellious or resigned—either way, he is threatened with spiritual ruin, for the dole is an evil, and idleness a curse. He soon becomes the seedbed of discontent, wrong thinking, alien beliefs. The Church cannot hope to save a man on Sunday if during the week it is a complacent witness to the crucifixion of his soul. (Quoted in Glen L. Rudd, *Pure Religion* [Salt Lake City: The Church of Jesus Christ of Latter-day Saints, 1995], 310)

Clearly there is a direct relationship between organizing ourselves such that temporal needs are met and saving ourselves spiritually. In a revelation to the Prophet Joseph Smith, the Lord boiled this concept down to a couplet: "And it is my purpose to provide for my saints. . . . But it must needs be done in mine own way; and behold this is the way that I, the Lord, have decreed to provide for my saints, that the poor shall be exalted, in that the rich are made low" (D&C 104:15–16).

Who are the poor? King Benjamin explained clearly in two separate verses that *all* of us are "poor" before God:

I say unto you that if ye should serve him who has created you from the beginning, and is preserving you from day to day, by lending you breath, that ye may live and move and do according to your own will, and even supporting you from one moment to another—I say, if ye should serve him with all your whole souls yet ye would be unprofitable servants. (Mosiah 2:21)

For behold, are we not all beggars? Do we not all depend upon the same Being, even God, for all the substance which we have, for both food and raiment, and for gold, and for silver, and for all the riches which we have of every kind? (Mosiah 4:19)

These verses tell us that none of us has the grace we need on our own to return to our Heavenly Father. Therefore, He has arranged for His Only Begotten Son, our elder brother, to give us that grace freely, even though we do not deserve it. We are saved spiritually on His merits, because we are all spiritual beggars.

Both those who are temporally poor and those who are temporally rich in this life can tend to forget that we are all spiritually needy. In order to help us remember our spiritual dependence, God has created us such that we have temporal needs for food, clothing, shelter, and health. These temporal needs are strong enough to drive change in individual and communal human behavior. These needs demonstrate our human weakness and should bring us to remembrance of our dependence on God.

When we have temporal needs, He has arranged for all of us to provide for one another, giving freely from our wealth to support each other—just as Jesus gives freely from His storehouse of spiritual strength. When we freely give, we are "made low," just as Jesus, who lived with spiritual wealth but descended below all things as He wrought the Atonement. Our temporal needs must be met so that we have the time in mortality that we need to prepare ourselves spiritually to return to God. Saints of God do not deny their brothers and sisters this temporal chance at eternal life.

There are many things that can go wrong in this life that can lead any one of us to be among the temporally poor. The circumstances and causes of these problems may differ, but the resulting agony and anguish are a shared human experience. It was relief from human anguish the prophet Jeremiah sought for his people:

> When I would comfort myself against sorrow, my heart is faint in me.
>
> Behold the voice of the cry of the daughter of my people because of them that dwell in a far country: Is not the Lord in Zion?
>
> The harvest is past, the summer is ended, and we are not saved.
>
> For the hurt of the daughter of my people am I hurt;
>
> Is there no balm in Gilead; is there no physician there? why then is not the health of the daughter of my people recovered? (Jeremiah 8:18–22)

We are not saved unless we have offered the balm of Gilead to all of God's children with whom we come in contact. The Lord intends to provide for all of the Saints, and I believe that means even "the weakest of all saints, who are or can be called saints" (D&C 89:3).

What I have learned by encountering dozens of people in many different circumstances of need is that the Lord cares for all of us. There *is* a balm in Gilead, and it is intended to improve every life, both temporally and spiritually. The Lord places no limits on what can be done when it is done His way. This means that the poor must be willing to be exalted and the rich must be willing to be brought low. That is His way.

In other words, those who are poor and who seek the help of the Lord must recognize and accept that the Lord's principle purpose is to help them by bringing to pass their "immortality and eternal life" (Moses 1:39), which is their exaltation. Temporal measures are simply a means to that end. Assistance with food, clothes, housing, health care, and other necessities is provided under inspiration from on high as a way to bring the recipients closer to God.

Many of the people I have assisted as a bishop are not members of the Church, and some have not expressed any religious interest at all. But as they have received assistance, I have always had teaching moments presented to me wherein I have testified of God's care. Temporal assistance, like the grace so freely given to all mankind through the Atonement, is rendered first as an invitation to learn to love God, to have faith in Him, and to comfort against sorrow.

These gifts from the Lord to each of us when we experience need are made possible as the rich are made low, meaning that they become humble enough to know that they too may someday find themselves in need temporally—and underscoring they are always in need spiritually. As we freely partake of the gift of grace from God, let us freely give, that the Lord's temporal storehouse may be full. This is how we collectively avoid finding that the harvest is past, the summer is ended, and we are not saved.

Latter-day servants of God, members of the Church of Jesus Christ, cannot take the gospel message throughout the world without having a rightful concern for human welfare; souls will not be saved if we witness their hunger, thirst, illness, joblessness, and poverty with complacency. Simply donating money does not fulfill the command to have charity; those who confine their contributions to money do not qualify for serving God, according to the fourth section of the Doctrine and Covenants. To that end, let us "pray unto the Father with all the energy of heart, that [we] may be filled with this love, which he hath bestowed upon all who are true followers of his Son, Jesus Christ" (Moroni 7:48). Charity is that love which typifies a disciple of Christ.

An Eye Single to the Glory of God

In a well-known passage of Mark Twain's novel *The Adventures of Huckleberry Finn*, Huck begins to worry that he is destined for "everlasting fire" as a punishment for helping the slave Jim to escape. The thought of eternal punishment makes Huck shiver, and he says:

> I about made up my mind to pray; and see if I couldn't try to quit being the kind of a boy I was and be better. So I kneeled down. But the words wouldn't come. Why wouldn't they? It warn't no use to try and hide it from Him. Nor from me, neither. I knowed very well why they wouldn't come. It was because my heart warn't right; it was because I warn't square; it was because I was playing double. I was letting on to give up sin, but away inside of me I was holding on to the biggest one of all. I was trying to make my mouth say I would do the right thing and the clean thing, and go and write to that nigger's owner and tell where he was; but deep down in me I knowed it was a lie, and He knowed it. You can't pray a lie—I found that out. (Ontario: Devoted Publishing, 2016, 99)

As Huck Finn says, you cannot pray a lie—but men and women have been trying to do that throughout religious history. Religious observances, such as prayer, were a nearly universal phenomenon in Jesus's time. Throughout Judea, people made a daily effort to comply with the religious observances of Mosaic law as tradition had embellished it. Jesus, though, was not impressed with overt religiosity. He reserved His sharpest criticisms for those who appeared devout but who were mostly unconcerned with really worshipping God. Speaking to the Pharisees, He said: "Ye pay tithe of mint and anise and cummin, and have omitted the weightier matters of the law, judgment, mercy, and faith: these ought ye to have done, and not to leave the other undone. Ye blind guides, which strain at a gnat, and swallow a camel, who make yourselves appear unto men that ye would not commit the least sin, and yet ye yourselves, transgress the whole law" (Joseph Smith Translation, Matthew 23:23–24). For Jesus, it matters not just whether you do the right thing but that you do it for the right reason.

During my mission to Austria as a young man, I learned that one of my companions went on a mission because his father promised to buy him a car if he served the whole two years. I also observed that some missionaries worked hard so that they received recognition for leading the mission statistics. During one particular week, as leader of a small group of missionaries, I induced my colleagues to distribute more copies of the Book of Mormon than any other group of Austrian missionaries. We received notoriety in the mission newsletter, but we were so intent with the effort to place the book, we relaxed our rules about bearing testimony to the truth of the book. We never taught the gospel to any of that week's recipients.

God has warned us many times against doing the right thing for the wrong reason:

> For behold, God hath said a man being evil cannot do that which is good; for if he offereth a gift, or prayeth unto God, except he shall do it with real intent it profiteth him nothing.
>
> For behold, it is not counted unto him for righteousness.
>
> For behold, if a man being evil giveth a gift, he doeth it grudgingly; wherefore it is counted unto him the same as if he had retained the gift; wherefore he is counted evil before God.
>
> And likewise also it is counted evil unto man, if he shall pray and not with real intent of heart; yea, and it profiteth him nothing, for God receiveth none such.
>
> Wherefore, a man being evil cannot do that which is good; neither will he give a good gift.

For behold, a bitter fountain cannot bring forth good water; neither can a good fountain bring forth bitter water; wherefore, a man being a servant of the devil cannot follow Christ; and if he follow Christ he cannot be a servant of the devil. (Moroni 7:6–11)

You cannot pray a lie.

It may seem harsh, but there is no halfway house to heaven. You cannot qualify to do God's work if you have your own agenda. "And faith, hope, charity and love, with an eye single to the glory of God, qualify him for the work" (D&C 4:5).

The phrase "an eye single to the glory of God" would have been identified by Joseph Smith with the words of Jesus on the Mount: "The light of the body is the eye: if therefore thine eye be single, thy whole body shall be full of light. But if thine eye be evil, thy whole body shall be full of darkness" (Matthew 6:22–23). The Greek word translated into the word *single* in Joseph Smith's Bible means "without guile." You cannot have schemes of your own and serve God. Jesus returned to that theme repeatedly:

> Take heed that ye do not your alms before men, to be seen of them: otherwise ye have no reward of your Father which is in heaven.
>
> Therefore when thou doest thine alms, do not sound a trumpet before thee, as the hypocrites do in the synagogues and in the streets, that they may have glory of men. Verily I say unto you, They have their reward.
>
> But when thou doest alms, let not thy left hand know what thy right hand doeth:
>
> That thine alms may be in secret: and thy Father which seeth in secret himself shall reward thee openly. (Matthew 6:1–4)

> And when he had called all the people unto him, he said unto them, Hearken unto me every one of you, and understand:
>
> There is nothing from without a man, that entering into him can defile him: but the things which come out of him, those are they that defile the man.

If any man have ears to hear, let him hear.

And when he was entered into the house from the people, his disciples asked him concerning the parable.

And he saith unto them, Are ye so without understanding also? Do ye not perceive, that whatsoever thing from without entereth into the man, it cannot defile him;

Because it entereth not into his heart, but into the belly, and goeth out into the draught, purging all meats?

And he said, that which cometh out of the man, that defileth the man.

For from within, out of the heart of men, proceed evil thoughts, adulteries, fornications, murders,

Thefts, covetousness, wickedness deceit, lasciviousness, an evil eye, blasphemy, pride, foolishness:

All these evil things come from within, and defile the man. (Mark 7:14–23)

For a good tree bringeth not forth corrupt fruit; neither doth a corrupt tree bring forth good fruit.

For every tree is known by his own fruit. For of thorns men do not gather figs, nor of a bramble bush gather they grapes.

A good man out of the good treasure of his heart bringeth forth that which is good; and an evil man out of the evil treasure of his heart bringeth forth that which is evil: for of the abundance of the heart his mouth speaketh." (Luke 6:43–45)

We are without guile and single in our eye toward God's glory when we work silently and unseen, without our left hand knowing what the right hand is doing, to accomplish God's work here on earth. Doing our good works before men where they can see us and give us credit leaves us short of the Christian standard. The glare of public acknowledgment will become our reward, our fifteen minutes of fame. What we do without others knowing is far more important than those things for which we take credit.

We cannot be made impure by the actions of others. Only we can determine our level of purity. What others can see us do does not determine our fitness before God because that fitness is determined within our hearts. Our friends and neighbors have only an indirect method for gauging our hearts; they can observe only the productivity of our lives. By our fruits we are known to them. But to God, we are known by the desires of our hearts.

Jesus often demonstrated His ability to see into the heart, to know what motivated the people around Him:

> And a certain ruler asked him, saying, Good Master, what shall I do to inherit eternal life?
>
> And Jesus said unto him, Why callest thou me good? None is good, save one, that is, God.
>
> Thou knowest the commandments, Do not commit adultery, Do not kill, Do not steal, Do not bear false witness, Honour thy father and thy mother.
>
> And he said, All these have I kept from my youth up.
>
> Now when Jesus heard these things, he said unto him, Yet lackest thou one thing: sell all that thou hast, and distribute unto the poor, and thou shalt have treasure in heaven: and come, follow me.
>
> And when he heard this, he was very sorrowful: for he was very rich.
>
> And when Jesus saw that he was very sorrowful, he said, How hardly shall they that have riches enter into the kingdom of God!
>
> For it is easier for a camel to go through a needle's eye, than for a rich man to enter into the kingdom of God.
>
> And they that heard it said, Who then can be saved?
>
> And he said, The things which are impossible with men are possible with God. (Luke 18:18–27)

Flattery is a sure sign that one's motivation is not pure before God. Jesus teaches us here to neither give flattery nor accept it. You cannot have your eye single to God's glory if you allow yourself to give or accept the glory for accomplishment without first acknowledging the source of all success, which is God. And you cannot be motivated as God is motivated, "to bring to pass the immortality and eternal life of man" (Moses 1:39), if there is anything you would withhold from God, keeping it to yourself when He asks you to give it up for Him. Given the enormous growth in personal wealth characteristic of the developed nations of the world during the past fifty years, it seems likely that middle-class citizens of today would possess greater wealth than the rich man of this New Testament story.

How shall we enter into the kingdom of God? Being saved is impossible for men and women who are without God in the world. But having an eye single to God's glory, willing to answer His call with a pure heart, we can forge our desires to become our passage to salvation.

Alma spoke of this as the "plan of restoration":

> And it is requisite with the justice of God that men should be judged according to their works; and if their works were good in this life, and the desires of their hearts were good, that they should also, at the last day, be restored unto that which is good.
>
> And if their works are evil they shall be restored unto them for evil. . . .
>
> The one raised to happiness according to his desires of happiness, or good according to his desires of good; and the other to evil according to his desires of evil; for as he has desired to do evil all the day long even so shall he have his reward of evil when the night cometh.
>
> And so it is on the other hand. If he hath repented of his sins, and desired righteousness until the end of his days, even so he shall be rewarded unto righteousness.
>
> These are they that are redeemed of the Lord; yea, these are they that are taken out, that are delivered from that endless night of darkness; and thus they stand or fall; for behold, they are their own judges, whether to do good or do evil. . . .

Do not suppose, because it has been spoken concerning restoration, that ye shall be restored from sin to happiness. Behold, I say unto you, wickedness never was happiness. . . .

All men that are in a state of nature, or I would say, in a carnal state, are in the gall of bitterness and in the bonds of iniquity; they are without God in the world, and they have gone contrary to the nature of God: therefore, they are in a state contrary to the nature of happiness.

And now behold, is the meaning of the word restoration to take a thing of a natural state and place it in an unnatural state, or to place it in a state opposite to its nature? . . .

This is not the case; but the meaning of the word restoration is to bring back again evil for evil, or carnal for carnal, or devilish for devilish—good for that which is good; righteous for that which is righteous; just for that which is just; merciful for that which is merciful.

Therefore . . . see that you are merciful unto your brethren; deal justly, judge righteously, and do good continually; and if ye do all these things then shall ye receive your reward; yea, ye shall have mercy restored unto you again; ye shall have justice restored unto you again; ye shall have a righteous judgment restored unto you again; and ye shall have good rewarded unto you again.

For that which ye do send out shall return unto you again, and be restored; therefore, the word restoration more fully condemneth the sinner, and justifieth him not at all. (Alma 41:3–7, 10–15)

If we do not desire to do good, meaning if we are not in synchrony with the desires of God, if our eye is not single to the glory of God, we will not do good. And if we live out our lives without God in this world, we cannot have happiness restored to us because it will be contrary to our nature to be anything other than wicked and unhappy. We will be our own judges, for we will know whether we belong with Jesus. That is why we cannot have mercy if we are not merciful, because we will become what we desired in our hearts throughout our lives. If we act mercilessly in this life, we will be without mercy in the next. You cannot pray a lie, and you will not live one in the next life.

Let us not praise each other for our service in God's kingdom. Consider that the laborer in Zion should wish to have his reward from God and not from men. Let us not seek a calling with a personal agenda. Let us not do good things because we otherwise feel guilty or shamed but because good deeds are a means to glorify God, whose only agenda is to bring about our immortality and eternal life.

Service to children is a hallmark of serving God with an eye single to His glory. Just when the disciples of Jesus were struggling with the concept of giving God the glory, Jesus taught that caring for children is equivalent to accepting Christ:

> At the same time came the disciples unto Jesus, saying, Who is the greatest in the kingdom of heaven?
>
> And Jesus called a little child unto him, and set him in the midst of them,
>
> And said, Verily I say unto you, Except ye be converted, and become as little children, ye shall not enter into the kingdom of heaven.
>
> Whosoever therefore shall humble himself as this little child, the same is greatest in the kingdom of heaven.
>
> And whoso shall receive one such little child in my name receiveth me.
>
> But whoso shall offend one of these little ones which believe in me, it were better for him that a millstone were hanged about his neck, and that he were drowned in the depth of the sea. (Matthew 18:1–6)

But the disciples were slow to learn this principle. Soon after Jesus had taught them to receive children, the disciples were caught trying to exclude children from the presence of Jesus: "Then were there brought unto him little children, that he should put his hands on them, and pray: and the disciples rebuked them. But Jesus said, Suffer little children, and forbid them not, to come unto me: for of such is the kingdom of heaven. And he laid his hands on them" (Matthew 19:13–15).

At the only moment known to us in scripture when Jesus experienced a fullness of joy to the point that He wept before the Nephite multitude, His response was to reach out to the children, bless them, and pray for them.

> Blessed are ye because of your faith. And now behold, my joy is full.
>
> And when he had said these words, he wept, and the multitude bare record of it, and he took their little children, one by one, and blessed them, and prayed unto the Father for them.
>
> And when he had done this he wept again;
>
> And he spake unto the multitude, and said unto them: Behold your little ones.
>
> And as they looked to behold they cast their eyes towards heaven, and they saw the heavens open, and they saw angels descending out of heaven as it were in the midst of fire; and they came down and encircled those little ones about, and they were encircled about with fire; and the angels did minister unto them. (3 Nephi 17:20–24)

These various verses make clear that contact with children can teach adults the characteristics of heavenly living, including humility, which is a beginning aspect of keeping our eye single to God's glory. Because of what children can do for us, we are commanded of Jesus to receive children, be with them, and serve them. Anyone who knows children will agree that children can easily spot phoniness or feigned interest. It is difficult to care for children while holding one's own agenda foremost.

Jesus lived by that principle. When children's needs were at stake, He took whatever time was necessary. At His moment of greatest joy, He thought first of children and arranged for them to be included center stage. If we are not likewise focused, if we avoid contact with children, if service to children is beneath our dignity, then we cannot have a fullness of joy with Christ because we do not share His priorities for blessing the lives of children. An eye single to the glory of God will always see to the needs of children.

The Apostle Peter once testified of Jesus that He "went about doing good" (Acts 10:38) and thereby was the means of publishing the word of God, beginning with the children of Israel. Jesus had no agenda other than doing the will of God. "Thy will be done," He said, "in earth, as it is in heaven" (Matthew 6:10). He repeated this same prayer at Gethsemane: "O my Father, if it be possible, let this cup pass from me: nevertheless not as I will, but as thou wilt" (Matthew 26:39). In between these two statements, Jesus taught through word and deed what is meant when He refers to the will of God:

> For I came down from heaven, not to do mine own will, but the will of him that sent me.
>
> And this is the Father's will which hath sent me, that of all which he hath given me I should lose nothing, but should raise it up again at the last day.
>
> And this is the will of him that sent me, that every one which seeth the Son, and believeth on him, may have everlasting life: and I will raise him up at the last day. (John 6:38–40)

Jesus freely gave His time and virtues to every person He met in life and freely gave His life for all men and women who have lived on earth. The will, work, and glory of God have the same object: to bring to pass the immortality and eternal life of God's children. If we are to have our eye single to the glory of God, we must go about doing good as Jesus did and have the same object in mind.

When the first group of Mormons arrived in Jackson County, Missouri, they desired to know the will of God concerning them as they began to live in what Joseph Smith told them was to become Zion. In answer came these words:

For behold, it is not meet that I should command in all things; for he that is compelled in all things, the same is a slothful and not a wise servant; wherefore he receiveth no reward.

Very I say, men should be anxiously engaged in a good cause, and do many things of their own free will, and bring to pass much righteousness;

For the power is in them, wherein they are agents unto themselves. And inasmuch as men do good they shall in nowise lose their reward.

But he that doeth not anything until he is commanded, and receiveth a commandment with a doubtful heart, and keepeth it with slothfulness, the same is damned. (D&C 58:26–29)

Any attempt to build Zion, to establish the kingdom of God on earth, will succeed only if the participants go about doing good, freely bringing to pass righteousness and anxiously engaging in the cause. We must learn what God's agenda is, leave our own agenda behind, and commit ourselves wholly to Him and His work and glory. If we withhold our energy from this work, wait until specifically commanded, and then doubt the wisdom of the command, we have our own agenda.

It is obvious from the Savior's life and Crucifixion that loving and forgiving others does not guarantee they will love you in return. We do not love and forgive in order to leverage a kind response from others. It seems paradoxical, but there are some things we can have only if we give them away. As Jesus pointed out, "Blessed are the merciful: for they shall obtain mercy" (Matthew 5:7). Mercy is one of those things we must give to others if we ever hope to have it ourselves.

Likewise, only the loving are truly beloved. Again, it is Jesus who articulates this principle: "For if ye love them which love you, what reward have ye? do not even the publicans the same?" (Matthew 5:46).

Forgiveness is the manifestation of charity that we must often give to those who curse, hate, persecute, and despitefully use us, without any expectation of a return. As such, forgiveness is a unilateral gift we give not because we expect our enemy to soften toward us but because we expect our efforts to forgive will soften our soul toward God.

The Savior taught this principle to the Church in Kirtland:

> My disciples, in days of old, sought occasion against one another and forgave not one another in their hearts; and for this evil they were afflicted and sorely chastened.
>
> Wherefore, I say unto you, that ye ought to forgive one another; for he that forgiveth not his brother his trespasses standeth condemned before the Lord; for there remaineth in him the greater sin.
>
> I, the Lord, will forgive whom I will forgive, but of you it is required to forgive all men.
>
> And ye ought to say in your hearts—let God judge between me and thee, and reward thee according to thy deeds. (D&C 64:8–11)

Forgiveness is ours only if we are forgiving. When we commit our lives to Christ, we make a unilateral promise to forgive all others, no matter what they do to us. The baptismal covenant is a promise to forgive. To violate that covenant is to harden ourselves such that we cannot be forgiven.

It is important to distinguish the command to unilaterally forgive all of our antagonists from our need to try to establish bilateral loving relationships within our sphere of influence. Christ provided instructions to us in these matters: "If thou bring thy gift to the altar, and there rememberest that thy brother hath ought against thee; leave there thy gift before the altar, and go thy way; first be reconciled to thy brother, and then come and offer thy gift" (Matthew 5:23–24).

We all must be forgiven, and our opportunity to enjoy God's forgiveness depends on our willingness to forgive our fellow men: "For if ye forgive men their trespasses, your heavenly Father will also forgive you: but if ye forgive not men their trespasses, neither will your Father forgive your trespasses" (Matthew 6:14–15).

As President Gordon B. Hinckley said, "May God help us to be a little kinder, showing forth greater forbearance, to be more forgiving, more willing to walk the second mile, to reach down and lift up those who may have sinned but have brought forth the fruits of repentance, to lay aside old grudges and nurture them no more" ("Forgiveness," Conference Report, October 2005). With President Hinckley, I pray that the blessings of forgiveness will permeate each of our souls.

As Huck Finn observed, you cannot pray a lie. And as Joseph Smith revealed, you cannot build Zion if you are not motivated by God's agenda. Having your eye single to the glory of God, being anxiously engaged, freely bringing to pass righteousness, exercising charity with a spirit of forgiveness—these are the essential qualifying features of the servant of God who goes about to do good.

REMEMBER

Peter's gradual conversion from fisherman to "fisher of men" is documented as an integral part of the New Testament narrative. Early in His ministry, Christ calls Peter to leave his nets and follow Him (see Matthew 4:18–20). Peter is an enthusiastic disciple with impulsive tendencies. He wants to follow Jesus, even as the Savior walks on water (see Matthew 14:25–31), but though bidden to do so, his fears overwhelm his faith and he sinks. He has a testimony of the redeeming mission of Jesus (see Matthew 16:13–20), revealed by the Spirit, but Peter does not initially have the courage of his convictions.

Peter cannot accept the Crucifixion, either on the road to Jerusalem or in the Garden of Gethsemane (see Matthew 16:21–28; 26:51–54). And when the conviction and Crucifixion of Jesus are actually taking place, Peter completely abandons his friend, denying he ever knew Him (see Matthew 26:69–75).

Peter witnessed the event on the Mount of Transfiguration (see Matthew 17:1–2), and he ran to see the resurrected Savior early that Sunday morning (see John 20:1–6), but when left leaderless, he reverted to catching fish (see John 21:3).

On and after the Day of Pentecost, however, his spiritual profile takes its final shape. Peter, with the companionship of the Holy Ghost, becomes a consistent source of spiritual strength. He knows how to testify to multitudes (see Acts 2:14). He is unafraid when imprisoned (see Acts 4 and 5), leading the Church through persecution. He sees into the hearts of Church members (see Acts 5:3). He recognizes revelation and implements it (see Acts 10:9–48). As he did personally, the whole church grows spiritually during Peter's ministry. While facing his own death with the courage he lacked at the time of Jesus's death, Peter reflects on his life and writes to the Saints about how to progress spiritually and why.

Peter teaches that one cannot remain at a spiritual standstill. Beginning with an initial faith in Jesus, or a love for Him and His gospel, we must work toward increasing spiritual capacity, or we will find ourselves losing spiritual ground. For those who never maintain an improving spiritual nature, Peter warns that they would have been better had they never had any faith at all: "For it had been better for them not to have known the way of righteousness, than, after they have known it, to turn from the holy commandment delivered unto them. But it is happened unto them according to the true proverb, The dog is turned to his own vomit again; and the sow that was washed to her wallowing in the mire" (2 Peter 2:21–22).

Peter's own experience with spiritual growth allows him to comment about the stepwise increase in spiritual capacity from faith to charity, which he recommends to ancient Christians:

> Whereby are given unto us exceeding great and precious promises: that by these ye might be partakers of the divine nature, having escaped the corruption that is in the world through lust.
>
> And beside this, giving all diligence, add to your faith virtue; and to virtue knowledge;
>
> And to knowledge temperance; and to temperance patience; and to patience godliness;
>
> And to godliness brotherly kindness; and to brotherly kindness charity.
>
> For if these things be in you, and abound, they make you that ye shall neither be barren nor unfruitful in the knowledge of our Lord Jesus Christ.
>
> But he that lacketh these things is blind, and cannot see afar off, and hath forgotten that he was purged from his old sins. (2 Peter 1:4–9)

When Joseph Smith received as revelation the answer to his father's inquiry in February 1829, now known as section 4 of the Doctrine and

Covenants, he was advised to "Remember faith, virtue, knowledge, temperance, patience, brotherly kindness, godliness, charity, humility, diligence" (verse 6).

Well-versed in the Bible, both father and son would have recognized this list as essentially from Peter's advice on how to stepwise advance one's spirituality. Rather than consider these attributes a nice but unconnected list, Joseph Smith and his father would have known that Peter had carefully selected and sequenced these as a means of instructing the Saints about service to God. It would not have been lost on Joseph Smith that he, like Peter, had begun his service enthusiastically only to falter when first encountering opposition. Joseph was probably grateful to have Peter's advice pointed out to him; it would have reassured him that he was not expected to become wholly spiritually mature overnight. Section 4 clearly indicates that we are qualified to serve God only upon acquiring faith, hope, charity, and an eye single to the glory of God. But verse 6 provides advice, by reference to Peter, about how to make that acquisition the work of a lifetime.

Peter's advice is that Jesus's divine atoning power has given us everything we need to succeed in life. In fact, Peter points out, through the glory and goodness of Jesus we are promised that we can escape our own corruption and evil desires in order to participate in the divine nature. Peter then explains how we can proceed in stepwise fashion to change our nature from corrupt to divine. To begin, Peter notes we must have faith, which we receive through the righteousness of our Savior. Because of the acts of Jesus, we have cause to believe that He can help us. In our need, Jesus offers His grace, which gift can initiate a loving relationship between each of us and Christ. This loving relationship is called faith and is the starting point for our spiritual transformation. Peter then advises that we should make every effort to act on our faith; in other words, we must be diligent in spiritual matters.

With our diligence we can add several attributes to our faith. By keeping the commandments of God, we can add virtue or goodness to our character. When we are obedient to a commandment of God, in addition to the good we do ourselves and others, we add knowledge of God, because we learn that diligence in keeping God's commands brings blessings. The blessings of God are a stark contrast to the consequences of impulsive behavior and sin, which bring us to the need for temperance or self-control.

Building character out of good habits requires patience, or perseverance, with which we can make a habit of virtue. We must apply ourselves to virtuous living for years. But as we are patient with this effort, our natures will begin to transform into something more like the character of Jesus. We will add godliness to our attributes; in other words, we will become more like Jesus.

The essence of Jesus's daily walk was His overriding concern for other people; He worried more about His brothers and sisters than He did about Himself. As we strive to be like Jesus, we add brotherly kindness to our attributes. Kindness repeated often over time becomes the true love of Christ, also known as charity. Thus, we begin by loving God, but by diligence, we ultimately learn to love like God.

Peter points out that without this transformation we will lose our love of God and will forget that He has offered us a remission of our sins. There is no spiritual spot for rest; we are either exercising our faith toward charity or we are losing our grip on God's grace.

Joseph Smith's shorthand version of Peter's advice on spiritual character building in section 4 adds humility to the list of attributes needed by the faithful. For Joseph, it is an important addition. He had been chastised the summer before because he boasted in his own strength (see D&C 3:4); he had become proud of his spiritual gifts. Pride is always at variance with both faith and charity. We cannot love either God or our fellow man if we love ourselves too much.

The state of blessedness described by Jesus at the beginning of the Sermon on the Mount is essentially a condition of humility. People who are poor in spirit, meek, mourning, hungering for righteousness, merciful, pure in heart, peacemakers, and persecuted all have something in common: they have come to a point in their lives where they desire something they know themselves powerless to create. They are prepared to rely on God.

I imagine that Joseph Smith, after seven months of heavenly silence following the loss of the translated manuscript, found consolation in this revelation and its reference to Peter's advice. In those seven months, Joseph very likely came to be poor in spirit, meek, and in need of mercy; he was likely hungering and thirsting to do righteous acts and mourning for his mistake in authorizing Martin Harris to borrow the manuscript. During this time, Joseph had also suffered the loss of a child, who died at birth.

Joseph humbled himself, came to the state of blessedness described in the Beatitudes, and was ready to learn from God. By reference to Peter, God taught Joseph to expect to make personal spiritual transformation an ongoing effort and not to expect instant success. As Joseph must have, let us each accept the assumption behind Peter's advice: if we apply ourselves and our faith, we can gradually acquire charity, the love of God.

The process of building character also calls on us to establish the habit of Sabbath-day worship, something by which we signify our effort. And in this, as in all other things, Jesus Christ set the unflinching example for us to follow. In our day, let us do what our Savior did and hallow the Sabbath as a sign between ourselves and our God.

Jewish Sabbath worship in synagogues likely began after the fall of Jerusalem and the destruction of the first temple. During the Babylonian captivity and under the leadership of the prophet Ezekiel, those who were in captivity were taught that their sins—including their failure to honor the Sabbath day—had weakened them and removed the protection of God from their homeland. Ezekiel recounted to his people the situation of the children of Israel, who "rebelled against [God]: they walked not in [his] statutes, neither kept [his] judgments to do them. . . . they polluted [the] Sabbaths," which caused God to "pour out [his] fury upon them" (Ezekiel 20:21). Hoping to spare his people the same punishment, Ezekiel taught them to hallow the Sabbath so that it would be a sign between God and His people (see Ezekiel 20:20).

Because of Ezekiel's warning, the Jewish people began to gather on the Sabbath to remember the covenant that had been made with Jehovah—a covenant they hoped to renew. Undoubtedly, Jesus, from a very young age, was raised to attend these Sabbath services, which had continued among the Jewish people even after a remnant had returned to Jerusalem and built the second temple. The New Testament makes it clear that Jesus never forsook that habit. In fact, Matthew wrote that "Jesus went about all Galilee, teaching in their synagogues, and preaching the gospel of the kingdom" (Matthew 4:23).

Early in His ministry, not long after his forty-day fast, Jesus attended Sabbath synagogue services in Nazareth. Perhaps because this was His hometown synagogue, He would have been assigned the reading from the scroll of the prophet Isaiah, and He went in order to fulfill that Sabbath teaching assignment.

When the moment for His reading came, He stood and read these words: "The Spirit of the Lord God is upon me; because the Lord hath anointed me to preach good tidings unto the meek; he hath sent me to bind up the brokenhearted, to proclaim liberty to the captives, and the opening of the prison to them that are bound" (Isaiah 61:1–2). Then, according to custom, He sat down before bearing a very short testimony: "This day is this scripture fulfilled in your ears" (Luke 4:21).

On another Sabbath, John recorded that Jesus taught a lesson that expanded on that testimony of salvation. Soon after the miracle of the loaves and the fishes, Jesus had taken His leave of the crowd quietly so as to avoid their growing desire for Him to assume a secular leadership role. The crowd then sought Him in Capernaum, where they found Him attending Sabbath services.

Jesus, knowing that the crowd had sought Him in order to receive more bread from Him, taught them to "labour not for the meat which perisheth, but for that meat which endureth unto everlasting life, which the Son of man shall give unto you" (John 6:27).

The crowd insisted that they wanted bread to eat, pointing out that God had provided manna from heaven for the people in the time of Moses. "And Jesus said unto them, I am the bread of life: he that cometh to me shall never hunger; and he that believeth on me shall never thirst.... For I came down from heaven, not to do mine own will, but the will of him that sent me" (John 6:35–38).

Jesus challenged the crowds to set aside their temporal concerns and to believe that He came from God, our Father in Heaven, to provide a way for God's children to receive the greatest gift of God—eternal life. Jesus then went on to teach a central lesson of the gospel, anticipating His eventual atoning sacrifice and the ordinance He would establish for all future Sabbath services:

> Then Jesus said unto them.... Except ye eat the flesh of the Son of man, and drink his blood, ye have no life in you.
>
> Whoso eateth my flesh, and drinketh my blood, hath eternal life; and I will raise him up at the last day.
>
> For my flesh is meat indeed, and my blood is drink indeed.
>
> He that eateth my flesh, and drinketh my blood, dwelleth in me, and I in him.
>
> As the living Father hath sent me, and I live by the Father: so he that eateth me, even he shall live by me.
>
> This is that bread which came down from heaven: not as your fathers did eat manna, and are dead: he that eateth of this bread shall live for ever. (John 6:53–58)

In this way Jesus taught His disciples that the work of salvation in the synagogue service held on the Sabbath was *personally* for them. He offered them eternal life as their personal Savior sent from their Father in Heaven upon condition of their choosing to believe in Him and repent.

All four Gospels include the story about the instigation of the sacrament as an ordinance for those who choose to follow Christ. Likewise, the Nephite prophets explicitly detailed the importance of Sabbath services and the sacramental ordinance in the spiritual lives of Christians. Moroni wrote:

> And after they had been received unto baptism, and were wrought upon and cleansed by the power of the Holy Ghost, they were numbered among the people of the church of Christ ... that

they might be remembered and nourished by the good word of God, to keep them in the right way, to keep them continually watchful unto prayer, relying alone upon the merits of Christ, who was the author and the finisher of their faith.

And the church did meet together oft, to fast and to pray, and to speak one with another concerning the welfare of their souls.

And they did meet together oft to partake of bread and wine, in remembrance of the Lord Jesus. . . .

And their meetings were conducted by the church after the manner of the workings of the Spirit, and by the power of the Holy Ghost; for as the power of the Holy Ghost led them whether to preach, or to exhort, or to pray, or to supplicate, or to sing, even so it was done. (Moroni 6:4–6, 9)

Modern-day prophets and Apostles have likewise taught us to remember the Sabbath day and to keep it holy, with particular attention to church services. Elder David A. Bednar taught: "That we might more fully keep ourselves unspotted from the world, we are commanded to go to the house of prayer and offer up our sacraments upon the Lord's holy day. . . . The sacramental emblems are sanctified in remembrance of Christ's purity, of our total dependence upon His Atonement, and of our responsibility to so honor our ordinances and covenants that we can "stand spotless before [Him] at the last day" ("Always Retain a Remission of Your Sins," Conference Report, April 2016).

The ordinance of the sacrament is a holy and repeated invitation to repent sincerely and to be renewed spiritually. In and of itself, the act of partaking the sacrament does not remit sins. But as we conscientiously prepare and participate in this holy ordinance with a broken heart and contrite spirit, the promise is that we may *always* have the Spirit of the Lord to be with us. And with the sanctifying power of the Holy Ghost as our constant companion, we can *always* retain a remission of our sins.

I have enough experience with prayerfully planning Sabbath-day services to know that these meetings are conducted according to the workings of the Spirit. When we follow the Messiah and accept assignments on Sunday to preach, pray, supplicate, or sing, we are doing the will of the living God. He has arranged for the priesthood to always be present to bless the emblems of His body and blood, thus ensuring that His blessings will keep you, His face will shine upon you, and His countenance will be lifted upon you.

In your quest for discipleship, attend the two hours of meetings so you can be nourished by the good word of God. Be numbered among the people of the Church of Christ on the Sabbath so that during the week you will keep in the right way and be continually watchful unto prayer.

Sabbath worship is designed to help you rely alone upon the merits of Christ. It is the work of our personal salvation. It is how you partake of the bread of life and thereby always retain a remission of your sins. On the Sabbath you will hear the preaching of good tidings. The brokenhearted are bound up, the captives are offered liberty, and the prisons are opened. By accepting the call to Sabbath worship, we receive the blessings promised by Isaiah to those who come to the Messiah: those who mourn shall have beauty for ashes, the oil of joy to transcend mourning, and the garment of praise for the spirit of heaviness (see Isaiah 61:3). They will become the trees of righteousness, the planting of the Lord.

Ask and Knock

The final verse of the fourth section of the Doctrine and Covenants reads: "Ask, and ye shall receive; knock, and it shall be opened unto you. Amen" (D&C 4:7). This is a final phrase of admonition from God to Joseph Smith Sr. through his son, the young Prophet, about serving God. The two men most likely also recognized these phrases as being from the Sermon on the Mount.

Matthew's account of the sermon reads:

> Ask, and it shall be given you; seek, and ye shall find; knock, and it shall be opened unto you:
>
> For every one that asketh receiveth; and he that seeketh findeth; and to him that knocketh it shall be opened.
>
> Or what man is there of you, whom if his son ask bread, will he give him a stone?
>
> Or if he ask a fish, will he give him a serpent?
>
> If ye then, being evil, know how to give good gifts unto your children, how much more shall your Father which is in heaven give good things to them that ask him? (Matthew 7:7–11)

Joseph Smith later revised this scriptural passage under inspiration, adding at the beginning: "Say unto them, Ask of God." In place of the verses about the response of a father to his son's requests, Joseph Smith through revelation provided four verses of conversation between Jesus and His disciples, as follows:

> And then said his disciples unto him, they will say unto us, we ourselves are righteous, and need not that any man should teach

us. God, we know, heard Moses and some of the prophets; but us he will not hear.

And they will say, We have the law for our salvation, and that is sufficient for us.

Then Jesus answered, and said unto his disciples, thus shall ye say unto them,

What man among you, having a son, and he shall be standing out, and shall say, Father, open thy house that I may come in and sup with thee, will not say, come in, my son; for mine is thine, and thine is mine. (Joseph Smith Translation, Matthew 7:14–17)

Joseph Smith already had the power of prayer validated by his own experience with seeing God. More than eight years before the revelation in section 4, Joseph had taken the biblical advice to ask God at face value and prayed for intelligence about joining a church. The answer on that occasion came directly from the mouth of God and began a lifelong lively conversation between Joseph and God's heavenly servants. All who enter into God's service are likewise admonished to begin and maintain a conversation with God. Faith, a relationship of love with God, depends on being on speaking terms with Him.

We do not pray, however, to tell God what to do or to tell Him what we need, for as Jesus pointed out, "Your Father knoweth what things ye have need of, before ye ask him" (Matthew 6:8). Rather, prayer is the work we do to bring our desires in alignment with God's intentions. When we have made enough effort through faith to acquaint ourselves with God, we begin to understand both what He intends to do for us and what small contributions we can make to His cause. That is the nature of any loving relationship: the two parties desire to help each other.

Faith, the loving relationship God invites us to have with Him, is nourished as we "work out [our] own salvation" (Philippians 2:12) with God by having words with Him. He speaks to us through His servants or through the Holy Spirit, and we organize our words back to Him in prayer. When we make enough effort to understand His words to us so that we can restate them in prayer, we have begun to internalize His message, and our prayers will achieve fruition.

Jesus said:

> Now ye are clean through the word which I have spoken unto you.
>
> Abide in me, and I in you. As the branch cannot bear fruit of itself, except it abide in the vine; no more can ye, except ye abide in me.
>
> I am the vine, ye are the branches: He that abideth in me, and I in him, the same bringeth forth much fruit: for without me ye can do nothing.
>
> If a man abide not in me, he is cast forth as a branch, and is withered; and men gather them, and cast them into the fire, and they are burned.
>
> If ye abide in me, and my words abide in you, ye shall ask what ye will, and it shall be done unto you. (John 15:3–7)

As Joseph Smith's inspired version of the Bible points out, however, many of us do not internalize God's word to us. Rather than shape our lives in accordance with His word and accept our need for His direction, we often shape His words to have a meaning convenient for us. By repeating someone else's prayer or by denying the possibility of receiving a direct communication from God, we make a lively conversation with God impossible, the failure of that communication a self-fulfilling prophecy. To say that God will not hear us or that we already have enough of His word is to insist that we must be sufficient unto ourselves or that God will not hear our words, when the problem is that we will not speak them to Him. The children of Israel failed their spiritual test in the desert because they refused to meet God face-to-face themselves (see Deuteronomy 5:5). They let their fears keep them from enjoying an intimate relationship with God. Prayer is our personal Mount Sinai.

The Lord does not simply instruct His servants to pray, He also instructs them to seek and knock. We cannot rest after we have discovered through prayer what the word of the Lord to us is. Said James:

> But be ye doers of the word, and not hearers only, deceiving your own selves.

For if any be a hearer of the word, and not a doer, he is like unto a man beholding his natural face in a glass:

For he beholdeth himself, and goeth his way, and straightway forgeteth what manner of man he was.

But whoso looketh into the perfect law of liberty, and continueth therein, he being not a forgetful hearer, but a doer of the work, this man shall be blessed in his deed. (James 1:22–25)

When we hear the word of the Lord in answer to our prayer, it is because we have done the necessary work to bring ourselves into alignment with God. God reflects His image of us back for our view. Whether we can retain the memory of that image depends upon what we do. If we fail to honor God's word in deed, we deceive ourselves by failing to live up to our spiritual privileges, and we forget our divine heritage as God's children. If, on the other hand, we are doers of the work, we will be knocking on our Father's door, and He will open it and share everything with us.

Contrast the state of mind that typifies the everyday common self-centered life with the state of blessedness Jesus describes in the Beatitudes at the beginning of the Sermon on the Mount:

Blessed are the poor in spirit: for theirs is the kingdom of heaven.

Blessed are they that mourn: for they shall be comforted.

Blessed are the meek: for they shall inherit the earth.

Blessed are they which do hunger and thirst after righteousness: for they shall be filled.

Blessed are the merciful: for they shall obtain mercy.

Blessed are the pure in heart: for they shall see God.

Blessed are the peacemakers: for they shall be called the children of God.

Blessed are they which are persecuted for righteousness' sake: for theirs is the kingdom of heaven.

Blessed are ye, when men shall revile you, and persecute you, and shall say all manner of evil against you falsely, for my sake.

Rejoice, and be exceeding glad: for great is your reward in heaven: for so persecuted they the prophets which were before you. (Matthew 5:3–12)

People who are prepared to take advantage of the healing the Christian gospel offers are meek, poor in spirit, merciful, seek peace, and hunger for righteousness. All of us are sinners, and we must remain primarily wallowing in that state until persuaded that we are miserable therein and that we just want relief—relief we cannot organize for ourselves.

The only alternative to the misery of this world is the state of blessedness Jesus here describes. It begins with a recommendation to be "poor in spirit," a state I would characterize as being tired, or emotionally exhausted, of carrying our worldly burdens of anger, pain, and self-sufficiency and wanting to do whatever it takes and to give up whatever we must (all pretense, all control, all desire to get even, all excuse) for the relief we seek. If we can get to that spiritual state, we would be in the state of blessedness Christ described and that is preliminary to enjoying the fruits of the Atonement, which is the manifestation of God's love for us.

If we do not feel the earnest need for being poor in spirit, mournful, meek, thirsty for righteousness, merciful, pure in heart, peaceful, and persecuted for righteousness, then we have work to do in prayer to our Father in Heaven. Our shortcomings and transgressions, the chaos of the world around us, the suffering of our brothers and sisters—all of these should leave us in a state of spiritual craving. We have, after all, suffered a spiritual death in coming to this world. We have left the presence of God. After Adam's transgression, God personally withdrew from the Garden of Eden, leaving behind a telestial sphere.

I believe it was this combination of humble craving for God's word that epitomized the prayer President Henry Eyring described in a sermon delivered in general conference:

Once . . . I prayed through the night to know what I was to choose to do in the morning. I knew that no other choice could have had a greater effect on the lives of others and on my own. I knew what choice looked most comfortable to me. I knew what outcome I wanted. But I could not see the future. I could not see which choice would lead to which outcome. So the risk of being wrong seemed too great to me.

I prayed, but for hours there seemed to be no answer. Just before dawn, a feeling came over me. More than at any time since I had been a child, I felt like one. My heart and my mind seemed to grow very quiet. There was a peace in that inner stillness.

Somewhat to my surprise, I found myself praying, "Heavenly Father, it doesn't matter what I want. I don't care anymore what I want. I only want that Thy will be done. That is all that I want. Please tell me what to do."

In that moment I felt as quiet inside as I had ever felt. And the message came, and I was sure whom it was from. It was clear what I was to do. I received no promise of the outcome. There was only the assurance that I was a child who had been told what path led to whatever He wanted for me. ("As a Child," Conference Report, April 2006)

Serving God requires us to have times of inner, quiet, humble moments when we desire only the state of blessedness Jesus taught about in His sermon. These are the moments when we are poor in spirit, aching for God to reach out and touch us because we know we depend on only Him. These are the moments when we actually mean that we will trade every material thing we have for God's comfort because we have learned that we cannot make ourselves comfortable here on earth. We are in a telestial sphere living outside of the presence of God, not in our natural spiritual environment. Not only that, but we have sinned and fallen short of the glory of God and no longer deserve to return to Him. We are twice removed from Him, and yet we long for His influence.

In the Book of Mormon, the father of King Lamoni, touched by the teachings of the Nephite missionary Aaron, also finds his spiritual Mount Sinai in prayer: "And it came to pass that when Aaron had said these words, the king did bow down before the Lord, upon his knees; yea, even he did prostrate himself upon the earth, and cried mightily, saying: O God, Aaron hath told me that there is a God; and if there is a God, and if thou are God, wilt thou make thyself known unto me, and I will give away all my sins to know thee, and that I may be raised from the dead, and be saved at the last day" (Alma 22:17–18).

In moments like these, we can take comfort in Jesus, who "came down from heaven, not to do [His] own will, but the will of [God]" (John 6:38). And as Jesus further explained, "And this is the will of [God] is that every one which seeth the Son and believeth on him may have everlasting life" (John 6:40). God's work, glory, and will is that we return to enjoy everlasting life with Him (see Moses 1:39).

For me, the times when I have stilled my selfish desires and subdued my own will, giving what I have to God, are the moments when I taste the goodness of eternal life. These are the moments when I understand the spiritual paradox that I must lose my life in order to find it (see Matthew 10:39). We must learn to let go of what appears to be ours in this life and humbly ask God for a gift according to His will, which gift is to exalt us.

I believe this is what is meant by the commandment to "offer a sacrifice unto the Lord thy God in righteousness, even that of a broken heart and a contrite spirit" (D&C 59:8). This is the spirit we should manifest at baptism and at the sacrament table. The commandment to ask and knock, bringing to God a broken heart and a contrite spirit, is at the cutting edge of spirituality for each of us. It is how we communicate with God and is therefore how we learn to be like Him:

> Behold, thus saith the Lord unto my people—you have many things to do and to repent of; for behold, your sins have come up unto me, and are not pardoned, because you seek to counsel in your own ways.
>
> And your hearts are not satisfied, And ye obey not the truth, but have pleasure in unrighteousness.
>
> Wo unto you rich men, that will not give your substance to the poor, for your riches will canker your souls; and this shall be your lamentation in the day of visitation, and of judgment, and

of indignation: The harvest is past, the summer is ended, and my soul is not saved!

Wo unto you poor men, whose hearts are not broken, whose spirits are not contrite, and whose bellies are not satisfied, and whose hands are not stayed from laying hold upon other men's goods, whose eyes are full of greediness, and who will not labor with your own hands!

But blessed are the poor who are pure in heart, whose hearts are broken, and whose spirits are contrite, for they shall see the kingdom of God coming in power and great glory unto their deliverance; for the fatness of the earth shall be theirs.

For behold, the Lord shall come, and his recompense shall be with him, and he shall reward every man, and the poor shall rejoice;

And their generations shall inherit the earth from generation to generation, forever and ever. (D&C 56:14–20)

ON TEMPLES AND TEMPLE LIVING

On July 23, 1833, barely eighteen months after arriving in Kirtland, Joseph Smith and the company of Saints living in Ohio laid the cornerstone of the Kirtland Temple. The building was to be sixty-five feet long and fifty-five feet wide, with two courts, or big rooms: the upper for a school of the prophets and the lower for worship meetings. Joseph clearly expected that the building would be nothing less than the best the Saints could produce.

The temple was completed in 1836 after nearly three years of labor. At the temple dedication, Church leaders David Whitmer and Frederick G. Williams both saw angels mingling with the assembled Saints during the seven-hour service. That night, many saw a pillar of fire resting on the temple.

The temple site in Independence, Missouri, had been selected in 1831, though the Saints there were driven out of Jackson County in 1834, before they had begun construction.

Less than two years after the dedication of the Kirtland Temple, Joseph Smith was forced to abandon Kirtland. He moved to Far West, Missouri, then home to five thousand Saints. There he laid the cornerstones for another temple. That temple was never built, however, because the Saints were forced to leave Missouri during the winter of 1838–1839.

Upon establishing a home for the Saints in Nauvoo, Illinois, Joseph again directed that a temple be built. However, he was martyred before the building was completed.

I have visited Kirtland, Independence, Far West, and Nauvoo. I have walked through the Kirtland Temple, stood on the abandoned Missouri prairie where the temple cornerstones of Far West are still visible, and attended an endowment session in the now-reconstructed Nauvoo Temple.

It is clear that Joseph Smith intended the Saints to draw spiritual strength from the temple. He instructed the elders in Kirtland to finish the temple and receive instructions there before leaving on their missions to the eastern United States. The Twelve Apostles were sent to Great Britain from Nauvoo but first took their leave of each other during a ceremony held at the abandoned temple site in Far West. The trek west from Nauvoo began only after the Saints brought the temple there to a sufficient state of completion so they could receive an endowment.

Today, we still follow the command to receive temple endowments before embarking on full-time service in the mission field. And like Joseph Smith, our current prophet carries on the temple-building process. Temple worship is central to Latter-day Saint living and is one of the unique aspects of our religion. As Joseph F. Smith revealed, the "great latter-day work" includes "the building of the temples" (D&C 138:53–54).

Temple worship was also central to life in ancient Israel, both in Jerusalem and among the Jewish transplants to the Americas chronicled in the Book of Mormon. Solomon built the house of the Lord on Mount Moriah on the site indicated by God, the traditional site of Abraham's altar where Isaac was spared. Solomon's temple was about the same square footage as the Kirtland Temple, though it was longer and narrower. It also had two rooms, or courts, called the Holy Place and the Most Holy Place or Holy of Holies. There were two decorative columns at the east end of the temple named Jachin and Boaz, meaning "God shall establish" and "In God is strength."

At the dedication of Solomon's temple, fire came down from heaven to consume the sacrificial offerings, and a cloud filled the house as the glory of the Lord was made manifest in Jerusalem. The Lord then put His stamp of approval on the structure: "The Lord appeared to Solomon . . . and said unto him, I have heard thy prayer and thy supplication, that thou hast made before me: I have hallowed this house, which thou hast built, to put my name there for ever; and mine eyes and mine heart shall be there perpetually" (1 Kings 9:2–3).

In Kirtland, a similar statement was made as the Lord appeared to Church leaders Joseph Smith and Oliver Cowdery a week after the dedication:

> For behold, I have accepted this house, and my name shall be here; and I will manifest myself to my people in mercy in this house.
>
> Yea, I will appear unto my servants, and speak unto them with mine own voice, if my people will keep my commandments, and do not pollute this holy house.
>
> Yea the hearts of thousands and tens of thousands shall greatly rejoice in consequence of the blessings which shall be poured out. . . .
>
> And the fame of this house shall spread to foreign lands; and this is the beginning of the blessing which shall be poured out upon the heads of my people. (D&C 110:7–10)

Several questions come to mind based on these observations and statements about two temples built by God's command nearly three thousand years apart. Why would God choose to live in an earthly edifice? For what reason would God direct us to sacrifice time and material to construct these buildings? More importantly, how does a modern-day Church member become one of the thousands and tens of thousands who greatly rejoice in the blessings of the temple?

Solomon himself wondered why God would choose to live in a building made by men. In his dedicatory prayer, which he pronounced while kneeling before the great altar of the temple, Solomon asked, "But will God indeed dwell on the earth? behold, the heaven and heaven of heavens cannot contain thee; how much less this house that I have builded?" (1 Kings 8:27). Why would God choose to sanctify a building made by mere mortals?

The dedicatory prayers of both King Solomon and the Prophet Joseph Smith contain insights about this question. Solomon prayed "that [God's] eyes may be open toward this house night and day . . . that [God might] hearken unto the prayers . . . of [His] people Israel, when they shall pray toward this place" (1 Kings 8:29–30). Solomon then went on to list several circumstances under which the people of Israel might turn to God in prayer, such as when they were suffering defeat, drought, famine, or captivity.

In each circumstance, Solomon noted that the cause of the problem was likely the failings of the people. He said:

> If they sin against thee, (for there is no man that sinneth not,) and thou be angry with them . . .
>
> Yet if they shall bethink themselves . . . and repent, and make supplication unto thee . . . saying, We have sinned, and have done perversely, we have committed wickedness;
>
> And so return unto thee with all their heart, and with all their soul . . . and pray unto thee toward . . . the house which I have built for thy name:
>
> Then hear thou their prayer and their supplication in heaven thy dwelling place, and maintain their cause,
>
> And forgive thy people that have sinned against thee, and all their transgressions wherein they have transgressed against thee, and give them compassion: . . .
>
> For they be thy people, and thine inheritance, which thou broughtest forth out of Egypt, from the midst of the furnace of iron:
>
> That thine eyes may be open unto . . . the supplication of thy people Israel, to hearken unto them in all that they call for unto thee." (1 Kings 8:46–52)

Likewise, as Joseph Smith dedicated the temple in Kirtland, he prayed "that all those who shall worship in this house . . . may grow up in thee, and receive a fulness of the Holy Ghost; . . . And when thy people transgress, any of them, they may speedily repent and return unto thee, and find favor in thy sight, and be restored to the blessings which thou hast ordained to be poured out upon those who shall reverence thee in thy house" (D&C 109:14–15, 21).

Clearly, a temple is a place where imperfect people can come to "grow up in the Lord." Members build temples to be a place where God can help them face the problems they create for themselves. The temple is a physical facility where God promises to perpetually keep His eyes and His heart, so He can see and feel the needs of His children. There He can manifest His mercy and save them from their own sins. The temple challenges the faithful to live according to God's commandments and gives them a sacred place wherein they can plead for themselves and for those they love. We go to the temple to be bathed in God's compassion. There we build spiritual momentum, turning to God with our entire heart and soul.

I have learned that I can be among the tens of thousands who rejoice in the blessings of the temple. In ancient Israel, there were fifteen steps leading to the first room, or Holy Place. Fifteen Songs of Ascent or Songs of Degrees were written so that an individual coming to the temple could sing or recite one on each step as he came up the steps. These fifteen Songs of Ascent are now known as Psalms 120–134. Each song in turn teaches a principle to live by so that, by degrees, the temple worshipper is brought to God.

I find that these songs, though written thousands of years ago, have direct application in my life. Psalm 120 advises me to call on the Lord when I am in distress, especially when my own failings have caused the problem. Psalm 121 answers that God will be my help: "He shall preserve thy soul" (Psalm 121:7). Others of these Songs of Ascent teach me that in the temple I will find God's mercy, that my children are my true heritage, and that I should strive to live together in unity with all God's children.

The final Song of Ascent reads: "Behold, bless ye the Lord, all ye servants of the Lord, which by night stand in the house of the Lord. Lift up your hands in the sanctuary, and bless the Lord. The Lord that made heaven and earth bless thee out of Zion" (Psalm 134:1–3). When I bless the Lord in His sanctuary, He will bless me in return. That is the essential promise of temple worship.

Despite these modern-day applications, temple worship in the latter days is obviously different in many respects from the ceremonies conducted in the temples of ancient Israel. Today, we believe we are blessed to officiate with the higher priesthood. In ancient Israel, the patrons were largely kept outside the sacred rooms of the temple. Only the priest went into the holy room, whereas today each person with a temple recommend is invited to pass behind the veil and visit the celestial room.

But current-day temple worship is still very much like the Songs of Ascent; in the temple, patrons are taught how they can raise their lives by degrees from mundane mortality in the telestial sphere to the blessings of celestial living. Those who attend carefully to temple worship in the fullness of times will learn how to remove Satan from their lives, how to take their lives from the telestial up to a new level of living in the terrestrial sphere, and how to speak intimately with God.

Because of the sacred nature of these teachings, I can only hint at this content. I do so only to illustrate the elevating nature of temple worship. *Light-mindedness*, an attitude we are counseled in the temple to shun, is not defined in our Bible Dictionary. The term is found only once in scripture, in the Doctrine and Covenants: "Therefore, cease from all your light speeches, from all laughter, from all your lustful desires, from all your pride and light-mindedness, and from all your wicked doings" (D&C 88:121). I once heard President Harold B. Lee state that he was not completely sure what the term *light-mindedness* meant, but he felt certain that making temple ceremonies the object of derision would fit the definition. What people are willing to laugh at tells something significant about them. A sense of humor about ourselves and the human condition can keep problems in perspective and lighten one's daily load. But too much levity may lead to light speeches, excess laughter, and light-mindedness.

We live in a world in which nothing seems sacred. Late-night comedians can make a joke out of anything. Sacred things, because they are connected to God and godliness, are consecrated, holy, and thus are worthy of reverence. They are set apart from the world for a purpose and must not be violated or disregarded. Things that are vulgar are not refined but are in poor taste. When nothing is sacred in life, everything is vulgar, lowbrow, and ignoble.

To be light-minded is to take nothing seriously, to find no cause in life worthy of special dedication. In such a state people will live down to lowered expectations and will be governed by the prejudices and interests of popular fashion. The vulgar sacrifice anything for pleasure or to get a laugh. Satan's interests are served by people enslaving themselves to vulgarity. If no part of life is reserved for special reverence, then Satan has access to everything in life. No wonder the temple teaches that people cannot remove Satan from their midst if they are light-minded.

The challenge of the temple is to live up to Peter's characterization of Saints: "But ye are a chosen generation, a royal priesthood, an holy nation, a peculiar people" (1 Peter 2:9). In the temple, we learn about what we've been chosen to do, what priesthood we should strive to magnify, and what holiness brings to our lives. In effect, we become a peculiar people by being a temple-living people. The direct result of temple living is the dismissal of Satan from among our society.

A similar leap forward in spiritual living is promised in the temple to those who live the law of chastity. No greater contrast exists in demonstrating the difference between true Christian living and vulgarity than comparing the blessings of chastity with the consequences of promiscuity. Modern people sneer at the societal pressures of a bygone era that required men and women to marry before exchanging sexual intimacy and that strictly forbade any other sexual expression. Such restrictions are now considered prudish, and unhealthy, even.

How ironic it is that the proponents of sexual liberty proclaim with certainty how beneficial it is for people, even at a young age, to satisfy coital appetites while they ignore epidemics of unintended pregnancy, sexually transmitted diseases, and mental illnesses characterized by anxiety and depression. In our headlong societal stampede to sexualize everything, we have horribly complicated our relationships. When intimacy is casual, it is no longer trusting or loving.

It is manifestly true that human happiness is not possible without truly loving relationships. The sexualized counterfeit of love, which now passes for romance in the popular and vulgar culture surrounding us, will never qualify as charity, the true love of Christ. No wonder we have a generation of unloved and unloving people, as predicted by the Savior: "And because iniquity shall abound, the love of many shall wax cold" (Joseph Smith—Matthew, 1:10).

Temple teachings are targeted against the tawdry sexual practices of today. The law of chastity is simple, and living thereby is uncomplicated. Virtuous living is less stressful, emotionally less complicated, and physically less risky. The difficult decisions of an unwanted pregnancy are not faced alone by a virtuous woman. Virtuous men never leave children without fatherly love and protection. The individual and societal burdens created by promiscuity are enormous and unnecessary. The temple teachings are right; if we lived the law of chastity, we would take our lives to a higher and better level, like going up one whole kingdom of glory.

A similar leap in glorious living is associated with the power of prayer—not just any kind of prayer but the kind we utter when we mean and care about what we say and are as anxious to listen to the answer as we are to say what is on our minds and in our hearts. Late BYU professor Truman Madsen wrote an essay about this kind of prayer:

> Humble prayer is the beginning of communion with the highest of personalities—God and his Son Jesus Christ—of higher ways of seeing and feeling, as it were, through their eyes. Achieving this is a life-process, not a five-minute thing. But it is sometimes closer in youth than in maturity. Youth may keenly grasp the truth: that even at our best we are like the blind boy who walks with his friend. He does not believe, nor bluff, that he is self-sufficient. Instead, he responds to the slightest nudge. (If you would know the power of God, try, early in life, to become just this dependable in your dependence.) As this happens, the whole being becomes the instrument that vibrates upwardly. No special words are needed,

no forced tone of voice, and no dramatic play-acting. (*Christ and the Inner Life*, 2nd ed. [Salt Lake City: Bookcraft, 1978], 16)

In contrast, Madsen says, we often offer "cool, bargaining, curious, all-talk-and-no-listen prayers." We pray

> for God to change everything—except us. . . .We hear much today about an identity crisis—the ache that comes when one begins to ask in a lonely, anguished way, "Who am I? What do I really want?" A lot of fuzzy answers can be given. But what is needed is a change of question. . . . You can kneel . . . and ask from the center of you, "Whose am I?" . . . When you expose your hidden self and latent faith and when you honor the quiet voice with total response, you will make a double discovery—yourself and God. That is what prayer is all about. (Ibid.)

True prayer brings you to a point where you can begin to see beyond the veil.

No matter where I stand in my life right now, I can begin to enjoy the blessings of temple living. Whether I must start outside the temple, like the entire nation of ancient Israel, or I already have a temple recommend and am privileged to ascend to the celestial room, I can enjoy the benefits of ascending by degrees into temple life. When I do so, I can join ancient Israel in praise of the house of the Lord. Said the Psalmist:

> One thing have I desired of the Lord, that will I seek after; that I may dwell in the house of the Lord all the days of my life, to behold the beauty of the Lord, and to enquire in his temple. (Psalm 27:4)

> My soul longeth, yea, even fainteth for the courts of the Lord: my heart and my flesh crieth out for the living God. . . .

> For a day in thy courts is better than a thousand [anywhere else]. (Psalm 84:2, 10)

ZION
THE NEW JERUSALEM

Among the Articles of Faith written by Joseph Smith is a promise about the future of the American continent that sets The Church of Jesus Christ of Latter-day Saints apart from other Christian religions: "We believe in the literal gathering of Israel and in the restoration of the Ten Tribes; that Zion (the New Jerusalem) will be built upon the American continent; that Christ will reign personally upon the earth; and, that the earth will be renewed and receive its paradisiacal glory" (Article of Faith 1:10).

A number of scriptures revealed by Joseph Smith support this prophetic statement. In the Book of Mormon, the prophet Ether, quoted by Moroni, stated that "after the waters had receded from off the face of this land it became a choice land above all other lands, a chosen land of the Lord; wherefore the Lord would have that all men should serve him who dwell upon the face thereof; . . . And that it was the place of the New Jerusalem, which should come down out of heaven, and the holy sanctuary of the Lord" (Ether 13:2–3).

Jesus Himself spoke of this promise during His sojourn with the Nephites in America after His Resurrection: "And behold, this people will I establish in this land, unto the fulfilling of the covenant which I made with your father Jacob; and it shall be a New Jerusalem. And the powers of heaven shall be in the midst of this people; yea, even I will be in the midst of you" (3 Nephi 20:22). Jesus went on to give a sign "that ye may know the time when these things shall be about to take place" (3 Nephi 21:1). He explained that the time for the fulfilling of this promise about the New Jerusalem shall be after the Gentiles, who will be set up as a free people, shall receive the Book of Mormon and learn of the Israelite origins of some American natives.

The use of the term *Gentile* in the Book of Mormon indicates people or nations who are without the fullness of the gospel, even though they may have some Israelite heritage. Christ indicates in this prophecy that these Gentiles will have a duty to bring the Book of Mormon to the descendants of Lehi. He further states that this Gentile role is provided so that the Gentiles may know God's power, be baptized, learn the true points of God's doctrine, and be numbered among the people of Israel.

The Book of Mormon context for this prophecy makes clear, at least in my opinion, that Jesus is speaking of Europeans, Africans, and Asians who come to America and partake in the Restoration of the gospel. In other words, he is talking about modern-day North Americans.

This is the time Isaiah foresaw. Speaking to Israel, he said:

> Enlarge the place of thy tent, and let them stretch forth the curtains of thy habitations; spare not, lengthen thy cords and strengthen thy stakes;
>
> For thou shalt break forth on the right hand and on the left, and thy seed shall inherit the Gentiles, and make the desolate cities to be inhabited. . . .
>
> For the mountains shall depart, and the hills be removed; but my kindness shall not depart from thee, neither shall the covenant of my peace be removed, saith the Lord that hath mercy on thee. . . .
>
> And all thy children shall be taught of the Lord; and great shall be the peace of thy children. . . .
>
> No weapon that is formed against thee shall prosper; . . . This is the heritage of the servants of the Lord." (Isaiah 54:2–3, 10, 13, 17; see also 3 Nephi 22:2–3, 10, 13, 17)

Joseph Smith and the earliest members of the Church thought about these prophecies a great deal and wanted to know more about them. In contrast, I believe that people today rarely think about these promises and consequently really do not understand them.

In June 1831, barely a year after the Church was organized and only a few months after the Saints' relocation to Kirtland, Ohio, the Lord designated that the next conference of the Church should be held in Missouri—then a frontier. He called fifteen pairs of elders to preach the gospel while wending their way to Missouri. He said, "If ye are faithful ye shall assemble yourselves together to rejoice upon the land of Missouri, which is the land of your inheritance, which is now the land of your enemies. But, behold, I the Lord will hasten the city in its time" . . . if "he that prayeth . . . [and] speaketh . . . is contrite" . . . and if the faithful "remember in all things the poor and the needy, the sick and the afflicted" (D&C 52:42–43, 15–16, 40).

Even though the land of inheritance was in the hands of their enemies, by September 1832, the Lord responded to inquiries from the Saints by inviting them to make an effort to build the city of Zion:

> Yea, the word of the Lord . . . for the gathering of his saints to stand upon Mt. Zion, which shall be the city of New Jerusalem. . . .
>
> Which city shall be built, beginning at the temple lot . . . in the western boundaries of the State of Missouri. . . .
>
> Verily, this is the word of the Lord, that the city New Jerusalem shall be built by the gathering of the saints, beginning at this place, even the place of the temple, which temple shall be reared in this generation. (D&C 84:2–4)

Ultimately this effort failed, and Joseph Smith said that the Lord pardoned the faithful members of the Church who were unable to fulfill the commandment to build the New Jerusalem:

> When I give a commandment to any of the sons of men to do a work unto my name, and those sons of men go with all their might and with all they have to perform that work, and cease not their diligence, and their enemies come upon them and hinder them from performing that work, behold, it behooveth me to require that work no more at the hands of those sons of men, but to accept of their offerings. . . .

Therefore, for this cause have I accepted the offerings of those whom I commanded to build up a city and a house unto my name, in Jackson county, Missouri, and were hindered by their enemies. . . .

And this I make an example unto you, for your consolation concerning all those who have been commanded to do a work and have been hindered by the hands of their enemies, and by oppression. . . .

For I am the Lord your God, and will save all those of your brethren who have been pure in heart, and have been slain in the land of Missouri, saith the Lord. (D&C 124:49, 51, 53–54)

At the time the Saints were expelled from Jackson County, however, Joseph Smith revealed that the Saints themselves had been deficient. In a revelation given at the Fishing River just after a thunderstorm had prevented an armed Missouri mob from attacking the small band of men known as Zion's Camp, the Lord said:

Were it not for the transgressions of my people . . . they might have been redeemed even now.

But, behold, they have not learned to be obedient to the things which I required at their hands, but are full of all manner of evil, and do not impart of their substance, as becometh saints, to the poor and afflicted among them;

And are not united according to the union required by the law of the celestial kingdom;

And Zion cannot be built up unless it is by the principles of the law of the celestial kingdom; otherwise I cannot receive her unto myself. . . .

Therefore, in consequence of the transgressions of my people, it is expedient in me that mine elders should wait for a little season for the redemption of Zion—

That they themselves may be prepared, and that my people may be taught more perfectly, and have experience, and know more perfectly concerning their duty, and the things which I require at their hands.

And this cannot be brought to pass until mine elders are endowed with power from on high. (D&C 105:2–5, 9–11)

The key instructions of this revelation then are given:

Talk not of judgments, neither boast of faith nor of mighty works, but carefully gather together . . . consistently with the feelings of the people;

And behold, I will give unto you favor and grace in their eyes, that you may rest in peace and safety . . . until the army of Israel becomes very great.

And I will soften the hearts of the people, as I did the heart of Pharaoh, . . . until Joseph Smith, Jun., and mine elders . . . shall have time to gather up the strength of my house. . . .

Let my army become very great, and let it be sanctified before me . . .

That the kingdoms of this world may be constrained to acknowledge that the kingdom of Zion is in very deed the kingdom of our God and his Christ, therefore, let us become subject unto her laws. (D&C 105:24–27, 31–32)

Since 1834, when Joseph Smith recorded section 105 of the Doctrine and Covenants, Church members have found themselves in this time of carefully gathering together and of growth in the army of Zion. They believe the Lord does indeed periodically soften the hearts of other peoples so that the Latter-day Saints may have favor and grace in their sight, allowing the necessary peace and safety.

The Saints must use this time wisely to learn to live the law of Zion. The Doctrine and Covenants is clear on this point: living the law of Zion requires being contrite in prayer and in speech, never boasting of faith. I take this to mean that Latter-day Saints must avoid the grievous sins of self-righteousness, pride, and boasting and must care for the poor, needy, sick, and afflicted, which means that they must help those with temporal and spiritual challenges. And they must sanctify their lives with temple worship. If they do these things, the sign that they are succeeding will be substantial growth in numbers. What Joseph Smith prophesied at Fishing River in Missouri was also seen by Isaiah and repeated to the Nephites by Jesus Himself.

I believe the importance of these Zion principles can, in part, be illustrated by the results of a sociological study that repeated a study done twenty years before. The new study found that 25 percent of Americans have no intimate friends—a rate twice that of two decades ago. In other words, one in four Americans has no one with whom he or she can discuss important matters, no one in whom to confide, no one with whom to share sorrows or to experience suffering. Another 25 percent of Americans have only one intimate friend. Half of American adults are lonely or are one friend away from loneliness. The average American has only two intimate friends, which is significantly fewer than twenty years earlier (Miller McPherson, Lynn Smith-Lovin, and Matthew E. Brashears, "Social Isolation in America: Changes in Core Discussion Networks over Two Decades," *American Sociological Review* 71 [June, 2006]: 353–75).

Here's what that means in practical terms: few people have friends they can turn to when in crisis, if they need child care, if they need help getting a medication, or if they need their mail brought in. America is nation trending toward personal loneliness, a trend that is in contrast to Zion.

Zion is strong because its people are on intimate terms with one another. They care about each other; they look out for the poor, needy, sick, and afflicted. Mormon describes the Zion society that flourished after the appearance of Christ among the Nephites:

> There was no contention in the land, because of the love of God which did dwell in the hearts of the people.
>
> And there were no envyings, nor strifes, nor tumults, nor whoredoms, nor lyings, nor murders, nor any manner of lasciviousness; and surely there could not be a happier people among all the people who had been created by the hand of God . . .

. . . but they were in one, the children of Christ, and heirs to the kingdom of God. And how blessed were they!" (4 Nephi 1:15–18)

What a contrast with the lonely state of affairs today.

Interestingly, it is this intimacy of personal relationships that makes Zion grow, at least according to sociologist Rodney Stark, who is not a member of the Church. Contrary to the general trends among Christian preachers today who seek for ever larger audiences—either through stadiums filled for revivals or vast radio and television broadcasts—conversion to faith occurs on a personal level. Large religious events tend to be attended by people who already have a belief, not those seeking to find new faith, much like the Super Bowl is meaningful to hardcore football fans but not the uninitiated.

Stark, who began publishing studies of the Church twenty years ago, has postulated that the Church would become a world religion in part because members of the Church were successful in including new people in their community. Put simply, people who are lonely are not primarily in need of doctrine—they are in need of a friend, or, better still, a network of friends.

For those living the gospel of Christ, it is second nature to help those around them. When neighbors need small favors, such as watering or feeding pets while they are away from home, these people respond. By these small acts, people become integrated into the lives of others and are less lonely. Over time, these acts bring people into each other's lives. As they become more intimate, they live the principles of Zion and strengthen their own neighborhoods (see Rodney Stark, *The Rise of Mormonism*, Reid L. Neilson, ed. [New York: Columbia University Press, 2005]).

These close, personal relationships are fertile ground for teaching the gospel. According to Richard G. Hinckley, former executive director of the Church Missionary Department, approximately 90 percent of those who listen to a message from members of the Church are first contacted by missionaries or Church media messages. But 60 percent of those who listen at length and who subsequently join the Church were found first among the friends of Latter-day Saints who only incidentally introduced them to gospel doctrine but who were practicing Zion principles, learning to love their neighbors.

When Joseph Smith told his fellow Latter-day Saints that the Lord said they must learn to impart of their substance, as becometh Saints, and be united in the cause of Zion, he was reiterating what has been said from the outset of the Church: much is required. Joseph Smith put it boldly: "A religion that does not require the sacrifice of all things never has power sufficient to produce the faith necessary unto life and salvation. . . . It is through the medium of the sacrifice of all earthly things that men do actually know that they are doing the things that are well pleasing in the sight of God" (*Lectures on Faith*, compiled by N. B. Lundwall [Salt Lake City: N. B. Lundwall, n.d.], 58).

President Gordon B. Hinckley has described the Church as "the most demanding religion in America," saying further, "and that's one of the things that attracts people to this Church." He later added: "[New converts] are put to work. They are given responsibility. They are made to feel a part of the great onward movement of this, the work of God. . . . They soon discover that much is expected of them as Latter-day Saints. They do not resent it. They measure up and they like it. They expect their religion to be demanding, to require reformation in their lives" ("What Are People Asking about Us?" *Ensign*, November 1998).

To an outsider, this may seem counterintuitive. Why would a church that demands so much be more attractive to the seeker of religion? Stark has a sociologist's answer for that paradox: Individual commitment increases the resources available for the religious congregation; increased resources mean that many things can be accomplished, which ultimately means that a religious community with high levels of member commitment has the greatest credibility concerning the promise of participation. Stark points out that the average ward receives four hundred to six hundred hours of voluntary labor each week, the equivalent of ten to fifteen full-time employees. This creates a huge, talented workforce to tackle not only leadership duties but the necessary functions of cleaning, clerical work, and administrative tasks. And after these jobs are done, there are plenty of volunteer hours to provide social services to one another, such as meals for families in distress, aid to the infirm, job counseling, and many other caring functions, Stark points out.

That is the sociologist's answer. The Lord, through Joseph Smith, said it far more simply: When you withhold your substance and are not united, you are not living the principles of Zion and cannot expect the promised New Jerusalem to materialize. In a sociologist's terms, a successful religion must generate a highly motivated volunteer religious labor force, sustain strong internal attachments within the group, and remain an open social network able to form ties to outsiders—all while making sufficiently strict demands to create a religious community that's a credible source of social strength. In prophetic terms: Zion cannot be built up unless it is by the principles of the law of the celestial kingdom.

If the Church succeeds at this, the Lord (through Joseph Smith) predicts a vast increase in the army of Israel "that the kingdoms of this world may be constrained to acknowledge that the kingdom of Zion is in very deed the kingdom of our God and his Christ" (D&C 105:32). Rodney Stark is much more prosaic in his prediction of enlargement of Church membership. Based on historical growth patterns, he predicts a worldwide Church membership of more than 50 million within my lifetime and more than 250 million within the lifetime of my children.

How do we prepare to be part of this vast increase in the army of Israel? How do we prepare to raise up young people ready to serve full-time, and how do we prepare to join in this missionary effort ourselves?

These questions were anticipated nearly three thousand years ago by prophets who lived during the Exodus and the scattering of the house of Israel. Moses was the sole prophet of the Exodus from Egypt; his story is well documented in the first five books of the Old Testament and is generally known by most. The second major movement, known as the scattering of Israel, is less well understood, in part because it took place over two centuries. While there were many prophets whose writings included information about the scattering of Israel, many of them are less well-known to members of the Church in the latter days.

Moses lived in about 1300 BC; the prophets of the scattering lived many years later, between 800 BC and about 400 BC. These prophets spoke and wrote extensively about the scattering of Israel, which they saw as the consequence of the wickedness of the people of Israel—both in the Northern Kingdom (where the ten tribes lived) and in the Southern Kingdom (where the tribe of Judah dominated). Make no mistake: these prophets were very disturbed about the things they were inspired to say. They feared the loss of the special covenants between Israel and the Lord forever. They themselves sought reassurance from the Lord about the preservation of these special covenants and the restoration of Israel.

One of the first of these prophets, Amos, lived and served God in the Northern Kingdom before its destruction and was a contemporary of Isaiah. Amos made it clear that the Lord was revealing everything relevant to the scattering of Israel through his prophets, saying, "Surely the Lord God will do nothing but he revealeth his secret unto his servants the prophets" (Amos 3:7). But the Lord also revealed through these same prophets many important secrets about the restoration of Israel. These instructions, of course, are important for us today as we live in the time of the gathering of Israel.

Of the scattering of Israel, Amos said:

> Woe to them that are at ease in Zion, and trust in the mountain of Samaria. . . .
>
> Therefore now shall they go captive. . . .
>
> The Lord God hath sworn by himself, saith the Lord God of hosts, I abhor the excellency of Jacob, and hate his palaces: therefore will I deliver up the city with all that is therein. . . .
>
> But, behold, I will raise up against you a nation, O house of Israel, saith the Lord the God of hosts; and they shall afflict you. (Amos 6:1, 7–8, 14)

The nation raised up against the kingdom of Israel was Assyria, with its capital in Nineveh, the city Jonah brought to repentance. Like all ancient conquering nations, Assyria was not able to sustain its own nation, and it eventually fell to the neighboring nation of Babylon.

For most of ancient history, Babylon—with its population about two hundred thousand—was the largest city in the world; it was probably the location of the Tower of Babel. It was located on the Euphrates River about fifty miles south of modern-day Baghdad, Iraq. Two of the seven wonders of the ancient world were in Babylon: the city wall—a double wall surrounded by a moat and consisting of two hundred and fifty towers; and the hanging garden, a mountain rain forest inside an arid city.

The streets of Babylon were paved with stone slabs that were three feet square. There were two massive golden images in the middle of the city—one of the god Baal and the other of a table. Each of these images weighed fifty thousand pounds and would be worth $1.3 billion each, given today's gold prices. In the midst of this was the great tower, probably built on the site of the Tower of Babel, called "House of the Platform of Heaven." This tower was three hundred feet high and was topped by a temple to the local god. Nebuchadnezzar's palace, also located in Babylon, was said to be unequalled in all human history.

Jeremiah, Ezekiel, Daniel, Lehi, Nephi, Nahum, Zephaniah, Obadiah, and Habakkuk were all living and prophesying just before or during the time of the Babylonian invasion of Jerusalem. The king of Judah, Zedekiah, was captured and forced to watch all but one of his sons be executed. (One of his sons, Mulek, escaped this fate and brought a group of people to the Americas, later joining the Nephites). After Zedekiah watched his sons' execution, he was blinded and brought captive to Babylon with most of the remnant of the Jews who had been living in Jerusalem.

Ezekiel, who had been serving among the priests of the temple, was among the captured people who were enslaved; he probably served on the massive public-works projects that made the wonders of Babylon. Daniel, who was of royal blood, was brought into Nebuchadnezzar's protection and trained up to be useful to the royal house of Babylon.

As all of this was occurring, the people of Israel wondered if they and their covenants with God would ever survive this catastrophe. Ezekiel gave voice to that concern:

> Then I fell down upon my face and cried with a loud voice, and said, Ah Lord God! Wilt thou make a full end of the remnant of Israel?
>
> Again the word of the Lord came unto me, saying. . . .
>
> Although I have cast them far off among the heathen, and although I have scattered them among the countries, yet will I be to them as a little sanctuary in the countries where they shall come. . . .
>
> Thus saith the Lord God; I will even gather you from the people and assemble you out of the countries where ye have been scattered, and I will give you the land of Israel.
>
> And they shall come thither, and they shall take away all the detestable things thereof and all the abominations thereof from thence.
>
> And I will give them one heart, and I will put a new spirit within you; and I will take the stony heart out of their flesh, and will give them an heart of flesh;
>
> That they may walk in my statutes, and keep mine ordinances, and do them; and they shall be my people, and I will be their God. (Ezekiel 11:13–20)

This is a great and concise formula for participating in the gathering of Israel: repent of your sins, get a new heart committed to God; love God with all your heart; keep God's commandments; and enter into covenants with Him.

While Ezekiel was preaching this formula for renewing the covenant of Israel and predicting a time when the gathering would come to pass, Daniel was helping King Nebuchadnezzar in the palace. The king had a dream that repeatedly came to him during the night. While the dream bothered him a great deal, he could not remember what the dream was. He summoned his wise men, but they were unable to help him. They promised to interpret the dream if the king would tell them what the dream was, but since the king could not remember the dream, all were frustrated. The king threatened to execute the wise men for being unable to help him with this dream.

It was into this threatening situation that Daniel came. He and his Jewish friends prayed for divine intervention, and then Daniel reported to the king:

> Thou, O king, sawest, and behold a great image. This great image, whose brightness was excellent, stood before thee; and the form thereof was terrible.
>
> This image's head was of fine gold, his breast and his arms of silver, his belly and his thighs of brass,
>
> His legs of iron, his feet part of iron and part of clay.
>
> Thou sawest till that a stone was cut out without hands, which smote the image upon his feet that were of iron and clay, and brake them to pieces.
>
> Then was the iron, the clay, the brass, the silver, and the gold broken to pieces together, and became like the chaff of the summer threshing floors; and the wind carried them away, that no place was found for them; and the stone that smote the image became a great mountain and filled the whole earth. . . .
>
> And in the days of these kings shall the God of heaven set up a kingdom which shall never be destroyed: and the kingdom shall not be left to other people, but it shall break in pieces and consume all these kingdoms, and it shall stand for ever.
>
> Forasmuch as thou sawest the stone was cut out of the mountain without hands, and that it brake in pieces the iron, the brass, the clay, the silver, and the gold; the great God hath made known to the king what shall come to pass hereafter: and the dream is certain, and the interpretation thereof sure. (Daniel 2:31–45)

Ezekiel and Daniel, both in Babylon, clearly prophesied a remarkable future event: the gathering of Israel and the establishment of the kingdom of God on the earth. As big and marvelous as was Babylon, what they saw in the future was much bigger and much better—and from an eternal perspective, it was also much more important.

These prophets, who were forced to watch the demise of their beloved Jerusalem and the destruction of the temple, had every reason to want to know whether and how the people of Israel would ever again enjoy God's blessings. They foretold the events in our day that would reestablish Israel, down to the details about how we, the children of Israel in the latter days, could participate in that great gathering.

The ancient prophets of Israel saw our day and knew that many of us would directly participate in the literal gathering of Israel and the establishment of the kingdom of God on the earth. They rejoiced in our day because they witnessed the destruction of Jerusalem and the temple in their own time. Our prophet is now calling upon us to take our places among the gatherers.

Those ancient prophets set the example for us in how we can prepare to participate in that great work.

We should be obedient, like Daniel, and refuse to defile ourselves with the temptations that surround us. And, like Daniel, we should perform our religious observances carefully and consistently. Darius, king of Babylon, issued a command that no one could pray to any god other than him—with a penalty of death for those who violated the command. Even knowing he faced death, Daniel continued to say his personal prayers. When Darius was forced to put Daniel in the lion's den overnight, Daniel, protected by the Lord, emerged unscathed the next morning.

We should avoid being like Jonah, who disobeyed the commandment of the Lord to preach repentance to the people of Nineveh.

We should follow Zechariah's counsel to "speak every man the truth to his neighbor; execute the judgment of truth and peace in your gates: and let none of you imagine evil in your hearts against his neighbor; and love no false oath" (Zechariah 8:16–17). People will follow our spiritual lead in these times of gathering if we are honest and fair to them and judge them and their works in good faith.

We must embrace the Book of Mormon as prophesied by Ezekiel: "The word of the Lord came again unto me, saying, moreover thou son of man, take thee one stick and write upon it, for Judah, and for the children of Israel his companions: Then take another stick and write upon it, for Joseph the stick of Ephraim, and for all the House of Israel his companions; and join them one to another into one stick; and they shall become one in thine hand" (Ezekiel 37:15–17). If we want to participate in the gathering of Israel, we must base ourselves, our choices, and our preaching on the scriptures of Judah and Joseph.

We must remember that temple work is the work of sanctification. If we want to be prepared to assist in the gathering of Israel, we need to be found in the temple.

We should honor the priesthood as taught by Malachi, the last prophet of ancient Israel. When we accept the oath and covenant of the priesthood, we promise to live such that we can be the messenger of God to His people.

We should recognize the great blessing of the Spirit Joel saw coming in our day (see Joel 2:28–32)—a prophecy reiterated by the angel Moroni to Joseph Smith where the Lord promises us, "I will pour out my spirit upon all flesh; and your sons and daughters shall prophesy, your old men shall dream dreams, your young men shall see visions: and also upon the servants and upon the handmaids in those days will I pour out my spirit" (Joel 2:28–29). Those who would serve the Lord in the gathering of Israel will need the gift of the Spirit to confirm their calling and prepare them for the rigors of His service.

As we teach the gospel, we must rely on the Spirit. All of us involved in the latter-day gathering will need that Spirit because, as Zephaniah prophesied, in our day we are surrounded by practical atheists—those who "say in their heart, the Lord will not do good, neither will he do evil" (Zephaniah 1:12). These "practical atheists" are people who believe in a God but do not believe God will actually act in their life.

In preparation for the gathering, we would do well to follow the example of Jeremiah, whose ministry lasted forty years during the most wicked time in Jerusalem—just before and during the Babylonian invasion. He was beaten, put in the stocks, imprisoned many times in wet and slimy conditions, and was eventually kidnapped and murdered. Despite all this persecution, he maintained the cause of the Lord: "The Lord's word was in mine heart as a burning fire shut up in my bones" (Jeremiah 20:9). We must live like Jeremiah and the other Old Testament prophets if we are to do the work of gathering they foresaw in our day. If we do, we will have a mighty change of heart, and the Lord will write His law in our hearts, "and will be [our] God, and [we] shall be [His] people" (Jeremiah 31:34).

Finally, Zechariah summed up our need for action in this day of gathering when he described the conditions in our day:

> I will strengthen the house of Judah, and I will save the house of Joseph, and I will bring them again to place them; for I have mercy upon them: and they shall be as though I had not cast them off: for I am the Lord their God, and will hear them.
>
> And they of Ephraim shall be like a mighty man, and their heart shall rejoice: Yea, their children shall see it, and be glad; their heart shall rejoice in the Lord.
>
> I will hiss for them, and gather them; for I have redeemed them: and they shall increase as they have increased.
>
> And I will sow them among the people: and they shall remember me in far countries; and they shall live with their children, and turn again.
>
> I will bring them again also out of the land of Egypt, and gather them out of Assyria; and I will strengthen them in the Lord; and they shall walk up and down in his name, saith the Lord. (Zechariah 10:6–10)

I have learned not to take the promise of a New Jerusalem for granted. I must bring my resources to the Lord's table and sacrifice them liberally. If membership in this Church has not extracted a price from me beyond the tithe, if I have not lost a worldly opportunity or two along the way, then I am not part of the experience of building Zion on this continent and will not be privileged to participate in the great work of the gathering.

CONSECRATE THINE AFFLICTIONS
FOR THY GAIN

During general conference, President James E. Faust gave a message of hope and counsel for people who wonder about the seemingly unfair distribution of pain, suffering, disaster, and heartache in this life ("Where Do I Make My Stand?" *Ensign*, November 2004). This theme reminds me of a story my wife told me about her adolescence.

My wife grew up in Orange County, California. Her house was on the edge of many acres of undeveloped hills covered with grass and low-growing shrubs. During a hot and dry period, a wildfire swept across the hills and approached the neighborhood. An evacuation was carried out during the middle of the night, and her family escaped with only their nightclothes, a pet, and a few pictures. Their house was one of perhaps a half dozen destroyed by the fire. A shift in the wind had prevented the wildfire from devastating the rest of the neighborhood.

A week or so after the fire exacted its damage, their ward held its regularly scheduled fast and testimony meeting. One of the neighbors whose house had not burned stood and bore testimony that God had answered his prayers and saved his house because he and his family had been keeping the commandments. You can imagine how that testimony affected my wife and her family.

I use this story to point out that traditional Christianity, and perhaps other religions, has adopted a rather simplistic view of the problem of evil and suffering in this world. This simplistic notion postulates that God is all-powerful and causes everything that happens in the world—meaning that nothing happens without God wishing it. A second notion postulates that God is just and fair and thus ensures people get what they deserve—which means that the good prosper and the wicked are punished. It follows from these simplistic propositions that people who have something bad happen to them must not be as worthy of God's blessing as people who enjoy good things in their lives.

Latter-day Saints are not immune to this error in thinking, as is illustrated by the testimony of my wife's neighbor after the wildfire. Another example of this kind of thinking among members of the Church came to my attention while I was serving as a missionary in Innsbruck, Austria. Located at the pulpit of the Church's chapel in Innsbruck is a large edition of the scriptures dedicated to two missionaries who died in an automobile accident on the freeway near the town. I overheard a discussion among my fellow missionaries about this event, where they were unified in thinking God was responsible for the tragic deaths of these two missionaries but were divided about why God caused this to happen. One group maintained that the missionaries must have been violating sacred covenants or otherwise breaking rules and so were not protected by God. The other group argued that God took the two missionaries for a higher purpose and to test their families who were left behind. My own view was that the two missionaries died in a car crash not because they violated God's law, but because somebody violated human traffic laws.

It should be apparent to anyone who thinks carefully about the premise that God is responsible for everything here on earth and therefore is responsible for all the suffering that occurs that the situation is not quite that simple. If people who happen to be righteous were always blessed and protected by God, what would keep them from violating with impunity such laws as the law of gravity? Why would they wait for the elevator when God would guarantee their safe arrival on the sidewalk no matter how high off the building they jumped? And if they were always rewarded with God's protection whenever they were righteous, how long would it take for everyone to get in line, thus frustrating the purpose of this life?

People who accept the simplistic notion that the righteous are protected and blessed by God and the wicked get what they deserve will inevitably have their convictions about God tested when problems occur in their lives. A large-scale example of the loss of faith that can occur when catastrophe harms apparently innocent people is the earthquake that occurred in the city of Lisbon, Portugal, on November 1, 1755—All Saints Day on the Catholic calendar. During the morning, when masses of people in the very devout city were assembled in their churches celebrating the holy day, a tremendous earthquake (that would likely have registered a nine on the Richter scale) rocked the city for five minutes. Gigantic fissures measuring five meters across opened up throughout the city's center. The massive cathedral collapsed, as did virtually all the other churches, killing thirty thousand devout citizens. Those who survived ran for the open safety of the docks at the port, where thirty minutes later a giant tsunami washed away thousands more.

The area of the city not inundated with the tsunami soon caught on fire. In all, ninety thousand citizens died that day out of a population of fewer than three hundred thousand. Approximately 85 percent of the buildings in the city were destroyed, as were the seventy-thousand-volume royal library; hundreds of works of art, including some by Rubens and Titian; and the royal archives, which contained the records and notes of Vasco de Gama and other explorers. Lost also throughout all Europe was faith in God.

Given the simplistic equation of many Christians that suffering occurs when God is not pleased, many people found God's apparent anger at the faithful Lisbon Catholics who died while attending to their church duties difficult to explain. For nearly a century after the catastrophe, European thought and faith was transformed toward agnosticism by rejection of a god who would bear responsibility for such great, undeserved suffering. No one seemed able to answer the question about why God would allow His children to endure so much pain and affliction.

President Faust gave a profound answer: "It's not so much what happens to us but how we deal with what happens to us" (Faust, "Where Do I Make My Stand?"). In other words, the proper question is not "Why do we have to endure this difficult problem?" or "Why did this happen to me?" but "What can I do when evil or suffering happens in my life?"

Lehi teaches this principle to his son Jacob just after they reach the promised land: "And now, Jacob, I speak unto you: Thou art my first-born in the days of my tribulation in the wilderness. And behold, in thy childhood thou hast suffered afflictions and much sorrow, because of the rudeness of thy brethren. Nevertheless, Jacob, my first-born in the wilderness, thou knowest the greatness of God; and he shall consecrate thine afflictions for thy gain" (2 Nephi 2:1–2).

If you think about it, Jacob had never known ease or comfort. He was born after the family left their prosperous life in Jerusalem, at a time when they were spending many years barely surviving in the Arabian desert. They had little to eat and were, on at least one occasion, near starvation. They had no permanent home and were either in the desert heat or subject to the storms on the high seas. Even worse, Jacob's older brothers were abusive to their family members, both physically and verbally. It was a harsh childhood and could have left emotional scars on Jacob. But his father helped him focus on the correct question—not "Why did these things have to happen to me?" but "How can I consecrate these afflictions for my gain?" Lehi advises Jacob as to how that can be done.

Lehi's first insights for Jacob explain that God is not the source of evil, affliction, and suffering in this world. Rather, Lehi points out that "men are instructed sufficiently that they know good from evil. And the law is given unto men. And by the law no flesh is justified; or, by the law men are cut off. Yea, by the temporal law they were cut off; and also, by the spiritual law they perish from that which is good, and become miserable forever" (2 Nephi 2:5).

In short, a most important source of suffering in this life is the poor choices people make. We harm ourselves when we make mistakes, and we may harm others as well. Jacob's brothers chose to torment their family members, making their lives miserable. In our day, when people fail to comply with traffic laws, serious injury to themselves or others can result. People usually know better than their performance would indicate.

Lehi goes on to indicate another source of affliction in this life:

For it must needs be, that there is an opposition in all things. If not so . . . righteousness could not be brought to pass, . . . having no life neither death, nor corruption nor incorruption, happiness nor misery, neither sense nor insensibility. . . .

Wherefore there would have been no purpose in the end of its creation. . . .

And if these things are not there is no God . . . [but] there is a God, and he hath created all things, both the heavens and the earth, and all things that in them are, both things to act and things to be acted upon.

And to bring about his eternal purposes in the end of man, after he had created our first parents, and the beasts of the field and the fowls of the air, and in fine, all things which are created, it must needs be that there was an opposition; even the forbidden fruit in opposition to the tree of life; the one being sweet and the other bitter.

Wherefore, the Lord God gave unto man that he should act for himself. Wherefore, man could not act for himself save it should be that he was enticed by the one or the other. (2 Nephi 2:11–16)

Opposition, including affliction, is a necessary component of this existence. It is built into the nature of this world. It is essential to the purpose of this life that we have death and all its antecedents, including injury and illness. This was the outcome of Adam's and Eve's choice in the garden of Eden. Moses describes this outcome as follows:

And I [God] will put enmity between [the serpent] and the woman. . . .

Unto the woman, I, the Lord God, said: I will greatly multiply thy sorrow and thy conception. In sorrow thou shalt bring forth children, and thy desire shall be to thy husband, and he shall rule over thee.

And unto Adam, I, the Lord God, said: Because thou hast hearkened unto the voice of thy wife, and hast eaten of the fruit of the tree of which I commanded thee, saying—Thou shalt not eat of it, cursed shall be the ground for thy sake; in sorrow shalt thou eat of it all the days of thy life.

Thorns also, and thistles shall it bring forth to thee, and thou shalt eat the herb of the field.

By the sweat of thy face shalt thou eat bread. (Moses 4:21–25)

In these verses, God describes this life as filled with enmity, sorrow, burdens, and ultimately death. Some affliction occurs just because of the nature of this world. An earthquake or a wildfire, for instance, may occur at any time and cause human suffering.

Finally, Lehi notes another source of affliction in this world: "And I, Lehi, according to the things which I have read, must needs suppose that an angel of God, according to that which is written, had fallen from heaven; wherefore, he became a devil, having sought that which was evil before God. And because he had fallen from heaven, and had become miserable forever, he sought also the misery of all mankind" (2 Nephi 2:17–18).

Suffering and affliction come to us in this world by these three means: people's poor choices, the nature of mortality, and Satan. God does not inflict suffering on us in this life, but because He has agreed to let us have our own opportunities to choose, He does not prevent the consequences of our choices from causing us to suffer. We chose to accept the parameters of a mortal life, including the risk of harm from nature, the choices of people, and the influence of Satan. We made this choice because we wanted a chance to grow, which mortality offers us. We should not now blame God when this life becomes difficult.

Lehi, however, does not just indicate that suffering and affliction are part of life. He teaches his son how to consecrate these problems to personal betterment. He begins by explaining how we can each be freed from the consequences of our own poor choices:

Wherefore, redemption cometh in and through the Holy Messiah; for he is full of grace and truth.

Behold, he offereth himself a sacrifice for sin, to answer the ends of the law, unto all those who have a broken heart and a contrite spirit; and unto none else can the ends of the law be answered.

Wherefore, how great the importance to make these things known unto the inhabitants of the earth, that they may know that there is no flesh that can dwell in the presence of God, save it be through the merits, and mercy, and grace of the Holy Messiah, who layeth down his life according to the flesh, and taketh it again by the power of the Spirit, that he may bring to pass the resurrection of the dead, being the first that should rise.

Wherefore, he is the firstfruits unto God, inasmuch as he shall make intercession for all the children of men; and they that believe in him shall be saved. (2 Nephi 2:6–9)

The Holy Messiah, being full of grace and truth, will intercede by His merits for us and save us from the consequences of our poor choices if we can break our hearts of the passion we have for the things of this world and become contrite in spirit. By saving us from the full consequences of our own mistakes, the Messiah makes possible our future presence with God, despite whatever we have wrongly done while separated from God in this life.

Lehi also teaches Jacob that the separation from God is necessary and that the effects of the fall from our innocent state in the premortal existence will be overcome:

And now, behold, if Adam had not transgressed he would not have fallen, but he would have remained in the garden of Eden. And all things which were created must have remained in the same state in which they were after they were created; and they must have remained forever, and had no end.

And they would have had no children; wherefore they would have remained in a state of innocence, having no joy, for they knew no misery; doing no good, for they knew no sin.

But behold, all things have been done in the wisdom of him who knoweth all things.

Adam fell that men might be; and men are, that they might have joy.

And the Messiah cometh in the fulness of time, that he may redeem the children of men from the fall. And because that they are redeemed from the fall they have become free forever, knowing good from evil; to act for themselves and not to be acted upon. (2 Nephi 2:22–26)

All those features of our current life that are inherent in mortality and that cause us to be subject to nature and the suffering associated with it are relieved by the life and actions of the Messiah.

Finally, Lehi identifies for Jacob the means for overcoming Satan's influence:

Wherefore, men are free according to the flesh; and all things are given them which are expedient unto man. And they are free to choose liberty and eternal life, through the great Mediator of all men, or to choose captivity and death, according to the captivity and power of the devil; for he seeketh that all men might be miserable like unto himself.

And now, my sons, I would that ye should look to the great Mediator, and hearken unto his great commandments; and be faithful unto his words, and choose eternal life, according to the will of his Holy Spirit;

And not choose eternal death, according to the will of the flesh and the evil which is therein, which giveth the spirit of the devil power to captivate, to bring you down to hell, that he may reign over you in his own kingdom. (2 Nephi 2:27–29)

Satan seeks to multiply our sorrows and afflictions into an eternal misery. But by the power of the great Mediator, who is the Messiah, Satan's influence over us is limited. He can only captivate those who do not choose to be faithful to the words of the great Mediator but instead choose to be ruled by the will of the flesh.

And so, as taught by Lehi, the three sources of affliction in this life are Satan, the fallen nature of this world, and the poor choices we and other people make. Each of these has an antidote, which is Jesus, the Messiah and the great Mediator of whom Lehi speaks. It is a great irony that many people, when faced with tribulation, cry out to God asking, "Why have you caused me so much suffering?" when in fact God is not the cause of suffering but has caused His Son to become the answer to all affliction.

There is usually not an answer to the question "Why must I suffer?" As President Faust noted: "As we live on earth we must walk in faith, nothing doubting. When the journey becomes seemingly unbearable, we can take comfort in the words of the Lord: 'I have heard thy prayer, I have seen thy tears: behold, I will heal thee' (2 Kings 20:5). Some of the healing may take place in another world. We may never know why some things happen in this life" (Faust, "Where Do I Make My Stand?").

We are here in a fallen state, partaking of a mortal experience and subject to suffering because we want to be here. We agreed to the conditions of suffering and affliction that we knew would be our lot. We can compound that suffering by making poor choices, which all of us are prone to do. When we follow the inclinations of the flesh, we give Satan an opportunity to make us even more miserable. These afflictions are not due to God's direct efforts to punish us. In order for us to exercise our agency, we must have options, and we must experience the consequences of our choices. God would rob us of this opportunity if He were to constantly intervene in our lives, alternatively dishing out punitive or provident moments for each action we take. Without real separation from God, we will never know if we will choose to be with God and seek Him above all other things.

As President Faust said, "We have much reason to hope. Joy can be ours if we are willing to sacrifice all for the Lord. Then we can look forward to the infinitely priceless possibility of overcoming all the challenges of this life. Then we will be with the Savior forever" (Faust, "Where Do I Make My Stand?"). Or as Lehi puts it: you know the greatness of God, "and he shall consecrate [your] afflictions for [your] gain" (2 Nephi 2:2).

If Any Man Will Come After Me

I find great comfort in the following verses in the Gospel of Matthew:

From that time forth began Jesus to shew unto his disciples, how that he must go unto Jerusalem, and suffer many things of the elders and chief priests and scribes, and be killed, and be raised again the third day.

Then Peter took him, and began to rebuke him, saying, Be it far from thee, Lord: this shall not be unto thee.

But he turned, and said unto Peter, Get thee behind me, Satan: Thou art an offence unto me: for thou savourest not the things that be of God, but those that be of men.

Then said Jesus unto his disciples, if any man will come after me, let him deny himself, and take up his cross, and follow me.

For whosoever will save his life shall lose it: and whosoever will lose his life for my sake shall find it.

For what is a man profited, if he shall gain the whole world, and lose his own soul? or what shall a man give in exchange for his soul?" (Matthew 16:21–26)

The Savior's uncharacteristically tough talk with Peter serves to emphasize the importance of this lesson concerning savoring the things of God more than the things of men, a lesson that also teaches us about the choice to gain either the world or one's soul. Apparently we cannot have both.

I believe that accepting Christ can inevitably lead to the loss of opportunity in the world. But those who cannot bring themselves to give up worldly opportunities forfeit something as well.

The price for a soul can be illustrated by the lives of two men born in pre-Victorian England. During the first half of the nineteenth century, Great Britain must have been an optimistic place. They had won the Napoleonic Wars in 1815, and the resulting trade opportunities in Europe were a windfall. The extensive network of rails connecting all parts of the kingdom was built in the 1830s, giving every town of size in the British Isles access to commerce. The Industrial Revolution had carried the British commercial class to new wealth, and Britain led the world in textiles, iron making, shipping, and military might.

Queen Victoria ascended the throne in 1837 and remained there for sixty-three years. During her reign, one-fourth of the world's people and land mass were ruled from London. Wealth poured into England from all over the world. With wealth came the opportunity for social reform, the striking down of brutal criminal laws, improving prisons, outlawing child labor, legalizing unions, and extending the vote to the middle class.

Yet amidst this prosperity, there developed a sense that something had been lost from civilized society. The great English poet Matthew Arnold, in a poem called "Dover Beach," captured that sense of loss:

The Sea of Faith

Was once, too, at the full, and round earth's shore
Lay like the folds of a bright girdle furl'd.
But now I only hear
Its melancholy, long, withdrawing roar,
Retreating, to the breath
Of the night-wind, down the vast edges drear
And naked shingles of the world.

Ah, love, let us be true
To one another! for the world, which seems
To lie before us like a land of dreams,
So various, so beautiful, so new,
Hath really neither joy, nor love, nor light,
Nor certitude, nor peace, nor help for pain;

And we are here as on a darkling plain
Swept with confused alarms of struggle and flight,
Where ignorant armies clash by night. (in *The Broadview
   Anthology of English Literature*, concise editing, volume B,
   Ontario: Broadview Press, 810)

Matthew Arnold was born in 1822, when the world of England did seem "like a land of dreams, so various, so beautiful, so new." He was reared by an energetic father who was a leader in both education and religion. It was Dr. Thomas Arnold who restored Rugby School to its pre-eminent place as a prep school for England's most brilliant students, most of whom went on to win first-class honors at Oxford or Cambridge. But he was not only headmaster of Rugby School—he was the leading voice calling for an end to strife among Christian religions and for a renewed devotion to simple Christian principles of living.

Matthew Arnold's mother was devoted to her nine children but did not overlook their faults. She loved each of them and made it very clear that they should live up to high principles, that hard work was expected, and that gainful activity should occupy their lives. In short, Matthew Arnold was blessed in his parentage and doubly blessed in the prosperity of his native land.

Yet at age twenty-two, Matthew Arnold concluded that there was no reason to believe in the Resurrection and Atonement of Jesus Christ. And so he would write that this world has "neither joy, nor love, nor light, nor certitude, nor peace, nor help for pain." And yet he wanted more from life. As a poet, he probably spoke for many of his era as he lamented in verse the emptiness of prosperity without heavenly purpose. His search for meaning in this life is crystalized for me in his poem "The Buried Life," which reads in part:

But often, in the world's most crowded streets,
But often, in the din of strife,
There rises an unspeakable desire
After the knowledge of our buried life;

> A thirst to spend our fire and restless force
> In tracking out our true, original course;
> A longing to inquire
> Into the mystery of this heart which beats
> So wild, so deep in us—to know
> Whence our lives come and where they go.
> And many a man in his own breast then delves,
> But deep enough, alas! None ever mines.
> And we have been on many thousand lines,
> And we have shown, on each, spirit and power;
> But hardly have we, for one little hour,
> Been on our own line, have we been ourselves—
> Hardly had skill to utter one of all
> The nameless feelings that course through our breast,
> But they course on for ever unexpressed.
> And long we try in vain to speak and act
> Our hidden self, and what we say and do
> Is eloquent, is well—but 'tis not true! (*Broadview Anthology*, 802)

For Matthew Arnold, there was no permanent relief from the disconnect between one's true nature and the person one portrayed in this world. The loss of faith experienced by Arnold and many of his generation proved to be a barrier to self-discovery. The only glimmers of hope he experienced, if we are to accept his poetry as testament to his soul, came when he learned to love someone else, as described at the end of "The Buried Life":

> Only—but this rare—
> When a beloved hand is laid in ours,
> When, jaded with the rush and glare
> Of the interminable hours,
> Our eyes can in another's eyes read clear,
> When our world-deafen'd ear
> Is by the tones of a loved voice caress'd—

A bolt is shot back somewhere in our breast,
And a lost pulse of feeling stirs again.
The eye sinks inward, and the heart lies plain,
And what we mean, we say, and what we would, we know.
A man becomes aware of his life's flow,
And hears its winding murmur; and he sees
The meadows where it glides, the sun, the breeze.

And there arrives a lull in the hot race
Wherein he doth for ever chase
That flying and elusive shadow, rest.
An air of coolness plays upon his face,
And an unwonted calm pervades his breast.
And then he thinks he knows
The hills where his life rose,
And the sea where it goes. (*Broadview Anthology*, 802)

At least nine of my ancestors lived in Great Britain during the first half of the nineteenth century, during the same time that Matthew Arnold lived there. Perhaps my ancestors, like their countryman poet, had "a thirst to [track their] true, original course" to find "whence [their] lives come and where they go."

One of my ancestors, George Jarvis, was born in 1823, and Ann Prior, his eventual wife, began her life in 1829. These two shared with Matthew Arnold the peace and prosperity of Great Britain during Queen Victoria's reign, though neither was born to the privileges Arnold enjoyed as a youth. They probably understood the spiritual unrest he wrote about. But they were blessed in a way he was not. This blessing had its origin in the United States.

In April 1839, Joseph Smith had only recently escaped unjust imprisonment in Liberty, Missouri. Governor Lilburn W. Boggs's Extermination Order allowing for the preemptive killing of Mormons was still considered valid. Most of the Latter-day Saints were bivouacked in Illinois, where they suffered terribly from disease, starvation, and exposure. But five of the twelve members of the Quorum of the Twelve Apostles were making their way surreptitiously across the state of Missouri to Far West. They, together with seventeen other faithful Saints, laid the foundation of a temple at Far West; then the five Apostles took their leave of the Saints en route to the mission field "over the great waters" to the British Isles.

The five Apostles traveled first to Nauvoo, Illinois, there to set in order their families' affairs before departing for Europe. All were destitute; none had adequate housing or a secure means for existence. Nonetheless, within months, all twelve Apostles were on their way to England. Here is the account of Brigham Young and Heber C. Kimball's departure by Church Historian B. H. Roberts:

> On the fourteenth of September, Brigham Young left his home at Montrose and started for England. He had been prostrated for some time by sickness, and at the time of starting on his mission was so feeble that he had to be assisted to the ferry, only some thirty rods from his house. All his children were sick, and he left his wife with a babe but ten days old, and in the poorest of circumstances, for the mobs of Missouri had robbed him of all he had. After crossing the river to the Nauvoo side, Israel Barlow took him on a horse behind him and carried him to the house of Elder Heber C. Kimball, where his strength altogether failed him, and he had to remain there for several days, nursed by his wife, who hearing that he was unable to get farther than Brother Kimball's, had crossed the river from Montrose to care for him. Four days later Elders Young and Kimball made another start. Elder Kimball left his wife in bed shaking with ague, and all his children sick. It was only by the assistance of some of the brethren that Heber himself could climb into the wagon. (B. H. Roberts, *Comprehensive History of the Church*, 2:23–24)

By the time most of these brethren returned to Nauvoo nearly two years later, the lives of my nine ancestors were about to be changed forever. Brigham Young made this entry in his journal on April 20, 1841:

It truly seemed a miracle to look upon the contrast between our landing and departing from Liverpool. We landed in the spring of 1840, as strangers in a strange land and penniless. But through the mercy of God we have gained many friends, established churches in almost every noted town and city in the kingdom of Great Britain, baptized between seven and eight thousand, printed 5000 books of Mormon, 3000 hymn books, 2,500 volumes of the *Millennial Star*, and 50,000 tracts, and emigrated to Zion 1000 souls, established a permanent shipping agency, which will be a great blessing to the Saints, and have left sown in the hearts of many thousands the seeds of eternal truth, which shall bring forth fruit to the honor and glory of God, and yet we have lacked nothing to eat, drink, or wear: in all these things I acknowledge the hand of God. (*Manuscript History of Brigham Young, 1801–1844*, Elden Jay Watson, comp. [Salt Lake City: Smith Secretarial Service, 1968]).

George Jarvis had been a sailor with the British navy since first enlisting at age seventeen. Having traveled all over the world with the navy—including trips to Australia, China, India, South Africa, Malay Islands, and the West Indies—George had returned home to England having been injured and found unfit for sea duty. He married Ann Prior in 1846.

In 1848, George met two elders from The Church of Jesus Christ of Latter-day Saints, Lorenzo Snow and Franklin D. Richards. He went home that night and told his wife "that an angel had appeared to Joseph Smith and that the church had been organized as it was anciently, and now missionaries were visiting the people, being sent out as the Apostles of Christ were." Ann listened intently to all he told her and then said, "George, it's true." They were baptized on Christmas Day, 1848, in the Thames River.

In Matthew Arnold's words, a bolt shot back somewhere in their breast and they knew. Their simple declaration of faith in 1848 was followed by more than half a century of arduous pioneering in Zion. They left England without enough resources to travel all the way to Utah, ending up in poverty in Boston for several years and then walking from

St. Louis to Salt Lake City, where Ann delivered my great-grandfather one month after their arrival in the valley.

One year later, George volunteered to join the first company of Mormon pioneers to settle in St. George, located in what is now Southern Utah. George and Ann found the faith that Matthew Arnold yearned for, each of them bearing testimony that they knew from whence their life came and where they were to go.

I love to read the poetry of Matthew Arnold. It has the power to express what is poignant about a life lived without faith in Christ. But I regret that Matthew Arnold never heard the clarion call of Christ from the missionaries who arrived in Great Britain after leaving their families in sickness and poverty in Illinois. I rejoice that my ancestors heard that message and immediately recognized what I have come to experience as truth. The message of the Book of Mormon is that, unlike Matthew Arnold, people do not need to live without God in the world. Faith is not receding from us, like an ebb tide on Dover Beach, but will grow within us and bless our lives.

Matthew Arnold sought earnestly for his buried life, but George Jarvis learned from the Book of Mormon prophet Alma that God gave us life in this world and desires to give us eternal life in a world to come. He learned from King Benjamin that joy and peace of conscience in this life are based on receiving a remission of sins through exceeding faith in Jesus Christ and that we must lose ourselves in the service of our fellow men.

In short, George Jarvis and my other eight British ancestors who were subjects of Queen Victoria gave up England in order to follow their faith, while Matthew Arnold kept his status in England and lost what faith he was born to. I join my ancestors in tracking my true original course, the one Matthew Arnold could not find in his own life. For, as the Savior said: "For whosoever will save his life shall lose it: and whosoever will lose his life for my sake shall find it" (Matthew 16:25).

GRACE

In the third chapter of Ephesians, we find the following:

That the Gentiles should be fellowheirs, and of the same body, and partakers of his promise in Christ by the gospel:

Whereof I was made a minister, according to the gift of the grace of God given unto me by the effectual working of his power.

Unto me, who am less than the least of all saints, is this grace given, that I should preach among the Gentiles the unsearchable riches of Christ; . . .

That Christ may dwell in your hearts by faith; that ye, being rooted and grounded in love,

May be able to comprehend with all saints what is the breadth, and length, and depth, and height;

And to know the love of Christ, which passeth knowledge, that ye might be filled with all the fulness of God." (Ephesians 3:6–8, 17–19)

I believe Paul has captured in these six verses what he meant when he said to the Corinthians that he was called to preach Christ crucified.

Those of us who have begun to know the dimensions of the love of Christ and the fullness of God are like Paul: we are given the task of ministering unto others that they may join with us in the body of Christ.

I have read some of the writings of a man who was called to preach Christ in Spain—and though he was not a Latter-day Saint, I believe he understood a great deal about the riches of Christ. His name was Dietrich Bonhoeffer, and he was born in Breslau, Germany, on February 4, 1906.

By age fourteen, Bonhoeffer had decided to become a minister in the Lutheran Church into which he had been born.

He began his university career at age seventeen, studying theology in Tübingen in Berlin and at the Union Theological Seminary in New York. He interrupted his study only once, at the age of twenty-one, to accept a call to serve a German congregation in Barcelona for a year. He published several theological treatises before his twenty-fifth birthday and began a promising career in academics as a lecturer in systematic theology at Berlin University at the age of twenty-four.

He preached often of the need for self-sacrifice and shared suffering. He said: "When a man really gives up trying to make something of himself—a saint, or a converted sinner, or a churchman (a so-called clerical something) a righteous or unrighteous man . . . when in the fullness of tasks, questions, success or ill-hap, experiences and perplexities, a man throws himself into the arms of God . . . then he wakes with Christ in Gethsemane. That is faith" (*The Cost of Discipleship* [New York: Collier, 1949], 24).

Bonhoeffer's faith was such that he could not abide the doctrines of National Socialism or its leader, Adolph Hitler. He repeatedly stood in opposition to the Nazis and actively worked for their defeat because they "strove to make history without God" (Bonhoeffer, 14). However, his faith also did not allow him to leave his countrymen. "I shall have no right," he said, "to participate in the reconstruction of Christian life in Germany after the war if I do not share the trials of this time with my people" (16). He was arrested and imprisoned in 1943 and executed without trial only a few days before Berlin fell in the spring of 1945.

Bonhoeffer published a book entitled *The Cost of Discipleship*, largely based on his own sermons delivered to his congregation in Spain. Bonhoeffer asks, "What did Jesus mean to say to us? What is his will for us today? How can he help us to be good Christians in the modern world?" (37). We could well ask an additional question: What riches of Christ are prepared for those who live two thousand years after Paul first preached the Crucifixion to the Mediterranean gentiles?

For Bonhoeffer, a key part of the answer is to understand what is meant by the term *grace*. Those who misunderstand the concept of grace opt for what Bonhoeffer calls "cheap grace":

> Cheap grace means the justification of sin without the justification of the sinner. Grace alone does everything they say, and so everything can remain as it was before. Cheap grace is not the kind of forgiveness of sin which frees us from the toils of sin. Cheap grace is the grace we bestow on ourselves. Cheap grace is the preaching of forgiveness without requiring repentance, baptism without church discipline, Communion without confession. Cheap grace is grace without discipleship, grace without the cross, grace without Jesus Christ.

Cheap grace is not what Paul meant when he referred to the riches of Christ.

Bonhoeffer contrasts this false notion of grace with the truth, which he calls "costly grace."

> Costly grace is the treasure hidden in the field; for the sake of it a man will go and sell all that he has. It is the pearl of great price to buy which the merchant will sell all his goods. It is the kingly rule of Christ, for whose sake a man will pluck out the eye which causes him to stumble; it is the call of Jesus Christ at which the disciple leaves his nets and follows him. Costly grace is the gospel which must be sought again and again, the gift which must be asked for, the door at which a man must knock. Such grace is costly because it calls us to follow, and it is grace because it calls us to follow Jesus Christ. It is costly because it costs a man his life, and it is grace because it gives a man the only true life. It is costly because it condemns sin, and grace because it justifies the sinner. Above all, it is costly because it cost God the life of his Son: "Ye were bought at a price," and what has cost God much cannot be cheap for us. Above all, it is grace because God did not reckon his Son too dear a price to pay for our life, but delivered him up for us. (47–48)

The price for true grace is difficult for all of us to pay. Bonhoeffer knew this:

> Are you worried because you find it so hard to believe? No one should be surprised at the difficulty of faith, if there is some part of his life where he is consciously resisting or disobeying the commandment of Jesus. Is there some part of your life which you are refusing to surrender at his behest, some sinful passion, maybe, or some animosity, some hope, perhaps your ambition or your reason? If so, you must not be surprised that you have not received the Holy Spirit, that prayer is difficult, or that your request for faith remains unanswered. How can you hope to enter into communion with him when at some point in your life you are running away from him? The man who disobeys cannot believe, for only he who obeys can believe. (72–73)

Obedience to the call of Christ is the price we must pay for His grace. The beginning of faith is to awaken with Jesus in Gethsemane—we must each accept our cup of bitterness, whatever it contains.

From the upper room where the Last Supper was held, Jesus led His Apostles in the dark across the brook Kidron to the Garden of Gethsemane, a name that means "olive press." There the scriptures record as follows:

> And they came to a place which was named Gethsemane: and he saith to his disciples, Sit ye here, while I shall pray.
>
> And he taketh with him Peter and James and John, and began to be sore amazed, and to be very heavy;
>
> And saith unto them, My soul is exceeding sorrowful unto death: tarry ye here, and watch.
>
> And he went forward a little, and fell on the ground, and prayed that, if it were possible, the hour might pass from him.
>
> And he said, Abba, Father, all things are possible unto thee; take away this cup from me: nevertheless not what I will, but what thou wilt. (Mark 14:32–36)

Even Jesus was amazed at the immensity of the price of the Atonement. In his Gospel, Luke said that blood poured from the Savior like sweat (see Luke 22:44). But the cup could not pass from Jesus, because if one person could withstand all evil, He could help the rest of us resist the smaller portions of evil we all face. Jesus later told Joseph Smith what this sacrifice cost:

> For behold, I, God, have suffered these things for all, that they might not suffer if they would repent;
>
> But if they would not repent they must suffer even as I;
>
> Which suffering caused myself, even God, the greatest of all, to tremble because of pain, and to bleed at every pore, and to suffer both body and spirit—and would that I might not drink the bitter cup, and shrink—
>
> Nevertheless, glory be to the Father, and I partook and finished my preparations unto the children of men. (D&C 19:16–19)

Meanwhile, Judas, having realized that Jesus would be staying this night in Jerusalem, went to inform the priests. This was the real treachery of Judas: providing the intelligence that Jesus would not be overnight in Bethany, where He had friends and safety. Judas probably took the priests first to the upper room and then, finding Jesus gone, to Gethsemane, where Jesus often spent time.

After His capture, Jesus was taken first to Annas, the previous high priest and father-in-law of Caiaphas, the then-current high priest. This was an illegal inquiry, as was the next, which occurred in the home of Caiaphas. Jesus was interrogated, which was also illegal—Jewish law required that legal cases were to be brought without requiring the accused to testify against himself and that the matter should be conducted in public, during business hours, in the court building. When Jesus protested, He was slapped across His face. The priests brought witnesses who could not agree with each other.

There were other illegalities: They tried Jesus on the eve of a Sabbath and a holy day. They bullied Him into making a statement. Further, the record is clear that the Sanhedrin had predetermined the verdict and wanted an excuse to extract capital punishment. After they convicted Him, they left Him until morning, when the Roman authorities would be available. They filled the time by blindfolding Him, hitting Him, and then taunting Him to prophesy who had hit Him. The next day the priests refused to go into the Roman Hall of Justice lest they make themselves unclean, undoubtedly the most hypocritical act recorded in scripture.

The priests knew the Romans would not execute Jesus for blasphemy, so they falsely accused Him of rebellion against Caesar. Pilate took Jesus into the Hall of Justice alone and asked:

> Art thou the King of the Jews?
>
> Jesus answered him, Sayest thou this thing of thyself, or did others tell it thee of me?
>
> Pilate answered, Am I a Jew? Thine own nation and the chief priests have delivered thee unto me: what hast thou done?
>
> Jesus answered, My kingdom is not of this world: if my kingdom were of this world, then would my servants fight, that I should not be delivered to the Jews: but now is my kingdom not from hence. (John 18:33–38)

Jesus asked Pilate the meaning of his question about Christ being king. When Pilate made it clear that he was only concerned about whether Jesus considered Himself to be a king of this world, Jesus explained that His was a spiritual leadership. Upon that testimony Jesus was acquitted.

The Jews were furious, and Pilate decided to send Jesus to Herod Antipas, puppet king of Galilee, who was in Jerusalem for Passover and who had previously killed John the Baptist. But Jesus refused to speak to Herod, who simply sent Him back to Pilate.

Because Pilate knew Jesus was innocent, Pilate wanted to appease the Jews by convicting Jesus of treason but then releasing Him as the traditional prisoner of leniency. But some of the same crowd that had hailed Jesus four days before as a Son of David now called for Him to die. At this point, Pilate's wife wrote to her husband this note: "Have thou nothing to do with that just man: for I have suffered many things this day in a dream because of him" (Matthew 7:19). Pilate subsequently washed his hands of the matter.

In those days, the first stage of a crucifixion was scourging, a brutal whipping intended to weaken the victim and shorten the time of death. During His scourging, Jesus was taunted with a crown of thorns by a Roman soldier. Pilate stepped in to stop the barbarism and for a third time tried to get Jesus off by saying, "I find no fault in him. The Jews answered him. We have a law, and by our law he ought to die, because he made himself the Son of God" (John 19:6–7). At that point, Pilate took Jesus back into the Hall of Justice alone and questioned Him again.

At about nine or ten o'clock that morning, Jesus was led away to Golgotha to be crucified.

At noon, the light of the sun was obscured. At three o'clock that afternoon, Jesus called with a loud voice, "My God, my God, why hast thou forsaken me?" (Matthew 27:46), which signaled a return of the solitary suffering that had happened in the garden. When that moment of intense suffering passed, Jesus knew His task was completed, and He chose to die, saying: "Father, into thy hands I commend my spirit" (Luke 23:46).

Immediately, an earthquake shook the earth, and the veil of the temple was rent. John the beloved testified that Jesus in fact did die on the cross: "But one of the soldiers with a spear pierced his side, and forthwith came there out blood and water. And he that saw it bare record, and his record is true: and he knoweth that he saith true, that ye might believe" (John 19:34–35).

Jesus died both a temporal and a spiritual death during His day of suffering. He alone was born with immortality, and He willingly gave up His life. He alone never separated Himself spiritually from our Father in Heaven, but God chose to leave Jesus alone in the garden and on the cross. Jesus went through the suffering He did so that "he descended below all things, in that he comprehended all things, that he might be in all and through all things, the light of truth" (D&C 88:6).

In dying, Jesus proved that the authority and power of this world is weak compared to the mightier power of loving people who think of others before thinking of themselves. All of us have chosen to remove ourselves from God; Jesus, by having the experience of God removing Himself, knows what we are going through. Said Alma:

> And he shall go forth, suffering pains and afflictions and temptations of every kind; and this that the word might be fulfilled which saith he will take upon him the pains and the sicknesses of his people.
>
> And he will take upon him death, that he may loose the bands of death which bind his people; and he will take upon him their infirmities, that his bowels may be filled with mercy, according to the flesh, that he may know according to the flesh how to succor his people according to their infirmities.
>
> Now the Spirit knoweth all things; nevertheless the Son of God suffereth according to the flesh that he might take upon him the sins of his people, that he might blot out their transgressions according to the power of his deliverance; and now behold, this is the testimony which is in me. (Alma 7:11–13)

This same testimony burns within my heart. For me, the power to endure the suffering of this life—with its pain, sickness, and infirmity—comes from the Atonement and death of Jesus. My testimony of Jesus is founded upon the forgiveness of sin I know He has brought to me. Because Jesus stood up to Caiaphas and Pilate, I know I can stand up for what is right, even if I am overwhelmed by worldly power. With one crushing blow to Satan, delivered in the Garden of Gethsemane and at Golgotha, Jesus purchased my return to God and overcame my physical and spiritual death.

Testimony and Conversion

During the course of my professional activities, I have, on a number of occasions, served as an expert witness in litigation. I am not a lawyer, but I am told there are standards a court should apply to determine whether a witness may provide testimony as an expert at a trial. The expert witness must have suitable experience or other qualifications beyond the average jury member's ability. As a physician, I have been asked to render opinions under oath about the nature of illnesses experienced by various people—particularly whether those illnesses could have been caused by exposure to chemicals or other potentially harmful substances in the individual's environment.

Generally, in order to render an expert opinion, I must make scientific observations about the problem using methods accepted by colleagues who have experience and training in the same field. In civil trials, the court usually requires me to pronounce that my scientific assertions in the matter are more likely than not to be the case; scientific certainty is generally not required for court testimony. In most cases, opposing lawyers will quiz me about opinions I have rendered in other sworn statements or published in the scientific literature. If my testimony on different occasions is found to be inconsistent, I am less likely to be believed by the jury.

My participation as a witness offering testimony under oath has led me to carefully consider what I mean when I stand and give testimony about spiritual matters. Most importantly, I have concluded that spiritual testimony is not a matter for experts only. Peter and John, who publicly healed the lame man at the temple (see Acts 3) were tried the next day by the high priest Annas and others for preaching about Jesus. They were found to be "unlearned and ignorant men," but their testimony was not disallowed because the Sanhedrin found "that indeed a notable miracle hath been done by them [and] is manifest to all them that dwell in Jerusalem; and we cannot deny it" (Acts 4:13–14, 16).

The high priest commanded Peter and John to not speak or teach in the name of Jesus, to which they replied, "Whether it be right in the sight of God to hearken unto you more than unto God, judge ye. For we cannot but speak the things which we have seen and heard" (Acts 4:18–20). Peter and John therefore established the principle that expert testimony is not required for spiritual matters, but that personal observation is the essence of a spiritual witness. This is an important principle. There is so much in this world that can be viewed only by a privileged few. Spiritual observations, on the other hand, are available to all without demographic or geographic limit.

Another important principle about spiritual testimony is that in spiritual matters, there is no separation of witness and judge. Mormon said:

> For behold, the Spirit of Christ is given to every man, that he may know good from evil. . . .
>
> And now . . . seeing that ye know the light by which ye may judge, which light is the light of Christ, see that ye do not judge wrongfully; for with that same judgment which ye judge ye shall also be judged.
>
> Wherefore, I beseech you . . . that ye should search diligently in the light of Christ that ye may know good from evil; and if you will lay hold upon every good thing, and condemn it not, ye certainly will be a child of Christ. (Moroni 7:16, 18–19)

The reason we have innate or inborn spiritual capacities—regardless of worldly education, wealth, experience, or location—is that God wants us to make our own judgments about good and evil. He wants us to be curious about our moral universe. He wants us to shine the Light of Christ in our lives and make spiritual observations about the things that matter most. Then He wants us to use those observations to judge for ourselves what is good. A spiritual testimony is, therefore, a statement we give about the goodness of God as we have observed it in our life.

As with expert testimony in a court, a spiritual testimony must be developed by effort made with an appropriate methodology. Mormon points the way toward this methodology: "And now . . . how is it possible that ye can lay hold upon every good thing?" he asks, meaning, how can you gain a testimony of the goodness of God in your life? He answers: "And now I come to that faith, of which I said I would speak; and I will tell you the way whereby ye may lay hold on every good thing" (Moroni 7:20–21).

Faith is the methodology of spiritual testimony. Alma explains: "Awake and arouse your faculties, even to an experiment upon my words, and exercise a particle of faith, yea, even if ye can no more than desire to believe, let this desire work in you" (Alma 32:27). This method of applying faith requires personal effort and observation. You must first choose what to believe, even if you can only desire to believe it. Then, with all your faculties, you must observe what happens as you act on that belief.

This is not a passive process; it requires our heart, might, mind, and strength. There is no spiritual witness that is simply given to us—we must actively acquire our testimonies. As God revealed to the Prophet Joseph Smith, "You have not understood; you have supposed that I would give it unto you, when you took no thought save it was to ask me. But, behold, I say unto you, that you must study it out in your mind; then you must ask me if it be right, and if it is right I will cause that your bosom shall burn within you; therefore, you shall feel that it is right" (D&C 9:7–8).

Like expert testimony in court, spiritual testimony does not need to be given with certainty. Alma explained that faith is not to have a perfect knowledge of things, but rather faith allows a gradual accumulation of information about spiritual reality. Alma asks, "O then, is not this real? I say unto you, Yea, because it is light; and whatsoever is light, is good, because it is discernible, therefore ye must know that it is good; and now behold, after ye have tasted this light is your knowledge perfect? Behold I say unto you, Nay; neither must ye lay aside your faith, for ye have only exercised your faith to plant the seed that ye might try the experiment to know if the seed was good" (Alma 32:35–36).

Unlike expert testimony in court, the experiments and observations leading to a spiritual testimony must not end as long as we live. We are not preparing to deliver a statement about a particular case on the day of trial in court, never to look at the file again. With spiritual testimony, the trial is our own; we will be the only witness and the ultimate judge. Our advocate is Jesus, but He can help us only if we have prepared our own testimony and can speak it with conviction.

The testimony that will matter will be a testimony that Jesus is our Redeemer, as recorded by Joseph Smith:

> That he came into the world, even Jesus, to be crucified for the world, and to bear the sins of the world, and to sanctify the world, and to cleanse it from all unrighteousness;
>
> That through him all might be saved. . . .
>
> This is the testimony of the gospel of Christ concerning them who shall come forth in the resurrection of the just—
>
> They are they who received the testimony of Jesus, and believed on his name and were baptized after the manner of his burial, being buried in the water in his name, . . .
>
> That by keeping the commandments they might be washed and cleansed from all their sins. (D&C 76:41–42, 50–52)

We begin to have a testimony of Jesus when we repent and receive relief from our sins through the grace of Jesus.

Those who "are not valiant in the testimony of Jesus" (D&C 76:79) are not allowed a celestial glory. The same thing is true for a spiritual testimony that is true when I render expert testimony in court—if I have not been consistent in sworn statements throughout my professional career, I will not be readily believed by a later judge and jury. Neither can I expect a fullness of spiritual blessings if my spiritual testimony is inconsistently applied.

The absolute requirements for lifetime consistency and effort to maintain spiritual testimony derive from the fact that the acquisition of a spiritual witness is not an end in itself, but rather a means to an end. It is well known that Peter had a testimony of Jesus prior to the Crucifixion:

> When Jesus came into the coasts of Caesarea Philippi, he asked his disciples, saying, Whom do men say that I the Son of man am?
>
> And they said, Some say that thou art John the Baptist: some, Elias; and others, Jeremias, or one of the prophets.
>
> He saith unto them, But whom say ye that I am?
>
> And Simon Peter answered and said, Thou art the Christ, the Son of the living God.
>
> And Jesus answered and said unto him, Blessed art thou, Simon Bar-jona: for flesh and blood hath not revealed it unto thee, but my Father which is in heaven. (Matthew 16:13–17)

Shortly after Peter expressed this conviction, he witnessed the transfiguration of Christ on the mount, surely another testimony-building event. However, just prior to His capture, Jesus spoke particularly to Peter and said, "Simon, Simon, behold, Satan hath desired to have you, that he may sift you as wheat: But I have prayed for thee, that thy faith fail not: and when thou are converted, strengthen thy brethren."

Peter's response seems almost impulsive: "Lord, I am ready to go with thee, both into prison, and to death."

Jesus, wanting Peter to know that all problems had been anticipated, responded: "I tell thee, Peter, the cock shall not crow this day, before that thou shalt thrice deny that thou knowest me" (Luke 22:31–34).

Peter's denial of Christ is well documented, as is his belief in the Resurrection upon finding the tomb empty and his meetings with the resurrected Lord in the closed room. Peter acquired several more spiritual testimonials—but still, when left to his own devices, he went back to fishing. Only after being admonished to feed Christ's sheep, after being taught for forty days, and after receiving the Holy Spirit on the day of Pentecost did Peter's ministry begin to take its final shape. Christ's prayer that Peter's faith would not fail until he was converted was answered.

We have a testimony when we have made one or more observations about the goodness of God in our lives. We are converted when we have consciously changed our nature from self-centered to God-centered. We become as Paul described conversion to the Corinthians:

> For we bear record that we are not beside ourselves; for whether we glory, it is to God, or whether we be sober, it is for your sakes.
>
> For the love of Christ constraineth us; because we thus judge, that if one died for all, then were all dead:
>
> And that he died for all, that they which live should not henceforth live unto themselves, but unto him which died for them and rose again.
>
> Wherefore, henceforth live we no more after the flesh; yea, though we once lived after the flesh, yet since we have known Christ, now henceforth live we no more after the flesh.
>
> Therefore if any man be in Christ, he is a new creature: old things are passed away; behold, all things are become new. (Joseph Smith Translation, 2 Corinthians 5:13–17)

The purpose of testimony is to whet our appetite for more direction from God—which, if we pursue, we will eventually desire to always be like God, never desiring anything else. That can be the work of a lifetime.

There is a danger when we become satisfied with the spiritual testimony experiences we have already enjoyed. We may stop striving for the next prompting, the next encounter with Christ, the next opportunity to serve. If we succumb to complacency after acquiring a testimony, we fail to realize the full promise of our spiritual beginning, even if we never deny what we have come to know. Such was the case for the Three Witnesses to the Book of Mormon: Oliver Cowdery, Martin Harris, and David Whitmer. Of them, BYU professor Richard Anderson writes:

By early 1838, disagreements on Church policies brought disaffection and excommunication for each of the Three Witnesses. . . . The alienation of the witnesses from the Church stemmed largely from conflicts regarding authority. After receiving revelation, the Three Witnesses felt they shared equally with Joseph Smith in foundational experiences, and their certainty about a past vision contributed to their inflexibility concerning future revelations. They sided with the Prophet's critics who reacted negatively to the failure of the Kirtland Safety Society, and they opposed Joseph Smith's vigorous doctrinal and administrative leadership. After their excommunication, each felt deep rejection, resulting, predictably, in their harsh criticisms of Church leadership. Even in these circumstances, each of the Three Witnesses continued to maintain vigorously the authenticity of their published testimony. None expressed any doubt as to what they had testified. Both Oliver Cowdery and Martin Harris returned to the Church at the end of their lives; David Whitmer retained religious independence but to the end aggressively defended the Book of Mormon." ("Book of Mormon Witnesses," in Daniel H. Ludlow, *The Encyclopedia of Mormonism* [New York: Macmillan Publishing Company, 1992])

While we can be grateful to the Three Witnesses for their stalwart stand concerning the Book of Mormon, perhaps their greater value is their example that no matter how much God reveals to us, we should be much more impressed with what we do not know. Mormon carefully advises us that we cannot have faith unless we are "meek, and lowly of heart" (Moroni 7:43). This is the blessed state described by Jesus in the Beatitudes (see Matthew 5:3–12; see also Luke 6:20–22). The poor in spirit, those who mourn, the meek, those hungering and thirsting for righteousness, the merciful, the pure in heart, the peacemakers, and the persecuted all have something in common: they know they are in need of God's help and are willing to wait on Him. They do not suppose themselves already endowed with certainty or a complete set of spiritual experiences.

Unlike the Three Witnesses, I have not seen an angel holding the gold plates while the voice of God confirmed that the translation made was true. However, I have held the Book of Mormon, read it many times, studied its doctrine, pondered its meaning, and prayed for spiritual enlightenment about it. I have come to feel that no other book better teaches the proper response to suffering; the nature of Jesus, the Son of God; or the meaning of the baptismal covenant.

I have learned to turn to the Book of Mormon for the strength to repent and to live by my righteous desires with faith, hope, and charity. I have found that Joseph Smith was prophetic when he said that the Book of Mormon would bring me closer to God than would any other book.

Because he brought that book to me, I have developed a profound interest in the life of Joseph Smith. I have walked where he walked in Vermont, New York, Ohio, Missouri, and Illinois. I have read biographies of his life and studied the revelations and teachings he recorded. I join with President John Taylor in celebrating the Prophet's life, believing that he has done more for my salvation than any other man, save Jesus only (see D&C 135:3).

As I have participated in the Church Joseph Smith established at the command of God—by serving as a full-time and stake missionary, worshiping in the temple, and attending to home teaching and other Church duties—I have come to believe myself a participant in the greatest movement in modern times: the effort to establish the kingdom of God on the earth.

My life has been blessed by the teachings initiated by Joseph Smith and preached directly to me by his successors, teachings that include tithing, fasting, Sabbath living, the Word of Wisdom, and many other principles. These feelings and discoveries of the goodness of God in my life are the foundation of my testimony, which I hope will be enhanced many times over in the coming years.

Most significantly, my spiritual life has been shaped by a desire to become a better person. I know I fail to live fully the love of God and fellow man that is the essence of Christianity. When my failings overwhelm me, I have repeatedly found reconciliation with God by believing in Jesus, the man who suffered all things so that He could show me and advise me how to succeed in this life. Because I have found relief in repentance through faith in Christ, I testify that Jesus has power given Him through His atoning sacrifice to lift each of us from the misery we often create for ourselves to the happiness we desire and strive to create. I pray I may have more spiritual experiences and that someday I may begin to understand the instinctual love Christ manifested for me during His life. I pray that my judgment may become more often like His so that I can respond as He would have responded. I believe that He believes I can be completely converted.

The Spirit Manifested in My Life

P aul begins his epistle to the Ephesians by thanking God, because he "hath blessed us with all spiritual blessings in heavenly places in Christ" (Ephesians 1:3). These spiritual blessings are key to our happiness here on the earth, as Paul explained to the Romans:

> For to be carnally minded is death; but to be spiritually minded is life and peace. . . .
>
> For as many as are led by the Spirit of God, they are the sons of God. . . .
>
> The Spirit itself beareth witness with our spirit, that we are the children of God: And if children, then heirs; heirs of God, and joint-heirs with Christ; if so be that we suffer with him, that we may be also glorified together. . . .
>
> Likewise the Spirit also helpeth our infirmities: for we know not what we should pray for as we ought: but the Spirit itself maketh intercession for us with groanings which cannot be uttered. . . .
>
> And we know that all things work together for good to them that love God, to them who are called according to his purpose. . . .
>
> If God be for us, who can be against us? . . .
>
> For I am persuaded, that neither death, nor life, nor angels, nor principalities, nor powers, nor things present, nor things to come,
>
> Nor height, nor depth, nor any other creature, shall be able to separate us from the love of God, which is in Christ Jesus our Lord. (Romans 8:6, 14, 16, 26, 28, 31, 38–39)

As Paul has said, the love God has for each of us that was manifested by Jesus our brother is made evident to us in this life by the Holy Spirit. Through the blessings of the Spirit we transcend above the material world and our carnal nature, and we taste the reality of God as we are able to inherit it. With the help of the Spirit, we can overcome our failings, organize our prayers to God, and recognize how God can help us transform our suffering into sanctification. If we can just learn to fulfill the promise of the sacramental prayers, that we "may always have his Spirit to be with [us]" (D&C 20:77), nothing ever will separate us from the love of God.

Until I was seventeen years old, I was unaware of the workings of the Holy Ghost in my life. At that time, I had begun to consider what course I might take after high school. I had had success both in school and on the football field. Consequently, a number of college football coaches had become interested in me. I had become particularly interested in the recruiting efforts of the U.S. Naval Academy. My mother's family had sent many of their sons either to West Point or Annapolis. The opportunity to receive a high-quality education while playing major college football appealed to me.

At that time, however, a commitment to one of the military academies made service in the mission field unlikely. My stake president had asked me whether I planned on serving a mission, to which I replied that I was likely to choose a career in the navy instead.

One Sunday, after preparing and blessing the sacrament, I listened to the speaker with unusual interest. Generally, I had not found much of serious interest during sacrament meeting. In fact, I cannot really recall any other speaker from that time in my life. So it was unusual that I found myself drawn to the speaker's words. He was reporting on his mission to Demark, which he had just completed. He spoke about the thrill of teaching the gospel and the meaning he had found in his own life while he worked among the Danish people. For some reason, I was fascinated by what he had to say.

Soon thereafter, I had a regularly scheduled interview with my bishop. He too asked me about potential service as a missionary, and I told him

I was seriously considering attending the U.S. Naval Academy. He then asked whether I had heard the remarks of the returned Danish missionary. I told him about my experience during that sacrament meeting—how the words of the missionary seemed to grab my attention, how fascinated I felt, and how unforgettable the experience was for me. My bishop looked me in the eye and told me that what I had experienced in that sacrament meeting was a gift of the Holy Spirit, and that through the Spirit the Lord was instructing me to prepare for missionary service.

As the bishop said that to me, I experienced a confirmation that what he was telling me was true. Somehow, in an undeniable manner, I knew he was right. This was the first time I recognized the power of the Holy Ghost. My thoughts were elevated, my purposes realigned, and I received insight beyond my own. I knew God cared about the decision I was making and, therefore, that He cared about me. I knew that the Spirit could help me focus my mind, sharpen my senses, and raise my performance.

Since that day, I have had many manifestations of the gift of the Holy Spirit in my life. I am most grateful for these spiritual gifts, especially because it is through the Holy Ghost that I received a witness that the Savior's Atonement can cleanse me from the effects of sin. When I am in need of guidance or find myself in difficulty, it is the Holy Ghost who can relieve me of anxiety, focus my faculties, assist me in my performance, and allow me to find relief from fear and failure. When under the influence of the Holy Spirit, I can let go of the things that matter less and be grateful for the things that matter most.

I have learned that spiritual gifts have predictable effects. Perhaps you have found, as I have, that these effects can help you reliably identify the workings of the Spirit in your life. The Holy Ghost always edifies me, always helps my mental performance. I always feel closer to my Father in Heaven when the Holy Ghost is present; I know better that He loves me and cares for me. The influence of the Spirit always induces me to be more thankful for the blessings I have.

I know better what to pray about and what to say to God in prayer when the Holy Ghost is present, and I am always inclined to pray when living spiritually. I understand more about the meaning of scripture, about the temple endowment, and about the words of the prophets when the Spirit is working with me. I am more able to love my brothers and sisters and act lovingly when I have the Holy Ghost with me. I am able to bear sadness and suffering with the Holy Ghost. Mundane Church assignments are transformed into blessings by the Holy Ghost.

By telling you these things about my experience with the Holy Spirit, I do not mean to imply that I rely on Him for all progress in my life. I know God will not arrange those things that are in my own power to accomplish. I know I will not receive an answer to prayer without making an initial effort to think through the problem myself. I know emotional situations are not necessarily fostered by the Spirit.

Each of us needs the sustaining influence of the Holy Spirit in our lives. The Spirit can assist us through our trials in private, sacred ways. The blessing of the gift of the Holy Ghost is what is promised us when we accept and keep the covenant of baptism and when we renew that covenant each week at the sacrament table. It is the Spirit that promises fulfillment of our deepest longings for God, our Father in Heaven.

THE GIFT OF HEALING

I graduated from medical school in 1982. A few weeks later I began my first assignment as an intern. I was assigned to the general pediatric service of the local children's hospital, where my duties were to evaluate and care for patients as they were admitted with injury or illness.

Shortly after arriving for my first day at work, I was informed I was on call for new admissions and that a seven-year-old boy with a sudden loss of consciousness would arrive later in the afternoon by helicopter. I met my new patient at the emergency room as he arrived with the transport team. His condition had worsened since the initial description of his illness had been radio transmitted from out of state, where his physician had called for the emergency service. The boy was in a deep coma. The initial evaluation was supervised by the attending neurologist, who was my team leader, and it documented that this child would not recover from this illness. We expected he would die that day.

The day had begun with great excitement for this seven-year-old boy. It was his birthday. His mother had planned a midday party, and he was ready for it. As the party began, however, he became unwell and confused. Ultimately, his mother had to cut the party short in order to take him to a physician. By the time they arrived at the doctor's office, the boy was difficult to arouse.

Recognizing a rapidly progressive central nervous system problem, the physician made arrangements for emergency transport to the children's hospital several hundred miles away. By the time I had this boy as my patient, we could hope only to keep him alive long enough for his mother to arrive by private car. When she did arrive and I gave her the unexpectedly awful news, she sobbed in anguish on her son's bed until his demise a short time later.

Contrast that painful scene with the following story taken from the Gospel of Mark:

> And, behold, there cometh one of the rulers of the synagogue, Jairus by name; and when he saw him, he fell at his feet,
>
> And besought him greatly, saying, My little daughter lieth at the point of death: I pray thee, come and lay thy hands on her, that she may be healed; and she shall live. And Jesus went with him; and much people followed him, and thronged him. . . .
>
> While he yet spake, there came from the ruler of the synagogue's house certain which said, Thy daughter is dead: why troublest thou the Master any further?
>
> As soon as Jesus heard the word that was spoken, he saith unto the ruler of the synagogue, Be not afraid, only believe.
>
> And he suffered no man to follow him, save Peter, and James, and John the brother of James.
>
> And he cometh to the house of the ruler of the synagogue, and seeth the tumult, and them that wept and wailed greatly.
>
> And when he was come in, he saith unto them, Why make ye this ado, and weep? the damsel is not dead, but sleepeth.
>
> And they laughed him to scorn. But when he had put them all out, he taketh the father and the mother of the damsel, and them that were with him, and entereth in where the damsel was lying.
>
> And he took the damsel by the hand, and said unto her, Talitha cumi; which is, being interpreted, Damsel, I say unto thee, arise.
>
> And straightway the damsel arose, and walked; for she was of the age of twelve years. And they were astonished with a great astonishment. (Mark 5:22–23, 35–42)

These two scenes have remarkable similarities: a child sick unto death, distraught parents who seek the aid of someone they trust. But the outcome is so different. Did God care for the daughter of Jairus but not the young boy who was my patient? Is the gift of healing an arbitrary thing, dependent on the presence of a particular spiritual master?

When I was seven years old, I experienced a death in my family. My brother was an infant, only two months old. One morning my mother went to wake him up because he had slept past his usual time; she found him dead in his crib. The cause was sudden infant death syndrome. My parents, too, were quite distraught—only for them, there was no possible appeal to some authority, medical or spiritual. They had not known that my brother was in any distress or at any risk.

Latter-day Saints are taught that the gift of healing, like all spiritual gifts, is possible for those who have faith:

> Seek ye earnestly the best gifts, always remembering for what they are given;
>
> For verily I say unto you, they are given for the benefit of those who love me and keep all my commandments, and him that seeketh so to do; that all may be benefited that seek or that ask of me. . . .
>
> For all have not every gift given unto them; for there are many gifts, and to every man is given a gift by the Spirit of God.
>
> To some is given one, and to some is given another, that all may be profited thereby. . . . To some it is given to have faith to be healed;
>
> And to others it is given to have faith to heal. (D&C 46:8–9, 11–12, 19–20)

Men who have been called and ordained to the priesthood are able to offer a blessing; such was the case for my father. But he was not aware his son was in distress.

Because I have been called and ordained to the priesthood and have spent many hours in hospitals, I have many times been asked by faithful members of the Church to set aside my profession and administer the ritual blessing of the sick. I am a believer in the power of those priesthood blessings, but the question still begs to be answered: Does God care only about the sick who have timely access to spiritual or medical healers?

My career has entailed various aspects of medicine and public health. The power to heal found within health-care delivery does require timely access. I have been at the bedside of an infant when that baby suffered a life-threatening episode of apnea (discontinued breathing), participating as part of the team of doctors and nurses in the newborn intensive care unit that saved the baby's life. Had my brother been where that kind of care was instantly available as soon as monitors alerted those around him that he was no longer breathing, he too would have survived. In that sense, healing through modern medicine is arbitrary. It happens only for those in the right place at the right time.

In the United States, we take health-care delivery seriously. We now spend almost 20 percent of the gross domestic product on health care—a total of $3 trillion per year. And the rate of spending on health care increases faster than the base rate of inflation every year. On a per capita basis, Americans are taxed more for health care than are the citizens of any other nation. And the total per capita spending in the United States is twice that of the average other first-world countries.

We do all this because we Americans do not want people to be arbitrarily without the health care they need—care that might save a life—and because there is a subtle hope that if we just try hard enough, do enough research, intervene with enough surgery, and administer enough medication, we will extend life, perhaps indefinitely.

Early in my medical training, I heard a professor state that there is no cause of death other than disease. And there is no disease that cannot be better studied and understood so that it can be cured. So, will the powerful technology of modern medicine make the gift of healing obsolete? Jesus was understood to have power over death. Can modern medicine equal that power?

I turn to scripture revealed by the Prophet Joseph Smith to answer these questions: "And I, the Lord God, formed man from the dust of the ground, and breathed into his nostrils the breath of life; and man became a living soul" (Moses 3:7; see also Genesis 2:7). There is no official doctrine of the Church, at least to my knowledge, that contradicts the basic tenets of modern biology concerning the evolution of species, including humankind. Personally, I accept Darwin's hypotheses as the best available explanation for biological diversity. What I do believe, and have been taught by Joseph Smith and all of his successors, is that it was God's plan to form the earth, populate it with living things, and place humankind, male and female, upon it. I find no contradiction between my belief in modern biology and in God as creator of the earth. Life is a gift from God—who, as King Benjamin observed, preserves us "from day to day, by lending [us] breath, that [we] may live and move and do according to [our] own will" (Mosiah 2:21).

Death has a different origin: "And I, the Lord God, commanded the man, saying: Of every tree of the garden thou mayest freely eat, but of the tree of knowledge of good and evil, thou shalt not eat of it, nevertheless, thou mayest choose for thyself, for it is given unto thee; but, remember that I forbid it, for in the day thou eatest thereof thou shalt surely die" (Moses 3:16–17; see also Genesis 2:16–17).

Death comes by way of the choices associated with our search for experience in this world. This experience, as painful and difficult as it always is, is meaningful and important to us. But it was intended to be short-term, and thus mortality is essential.

"And I, the Lord God, said unto mine Only Begotten: Behold, the man is become as one of us to know good and evil; and now lest he put forth his hand and partake also of the tree of life, and eat and live forever, therefore I, the Lord God, will send him forth from the Garden of Eden, to till the ground from whence he was taken. . . . So I drove out the man, and I placed at the east of the Garden of Eden, cherubim and a flaming sword, which turned every way to keep the way of the tree of life" (Moses 4:28–29, 31; see also Genesis 3:22–24).

With these words, Joseph Smith predicts a limit to the success of modern medicine. The way of the tree of life, and therefore endless health, is known only to God. Disease and death will eventually come to every man and woman, and there are no arbitrary exceptions.

As a physician, I have come to realize the limits of the science and craft of my profession. No matter what startling new possibilities seem to be on the surgical or pharmaceutical horizon, we are bound by the philosophical origins of our technological healing efforts. At the root of medical science is a metaphor, a useful assumption, that we can treat the human body as if it were a machine. For the purposes of understanding our body and the afflictions that torment it, this metaphor is clever and powerful. But it is not the complete truth. It is merely a metaphor—and, as such, it does not have the power to make us immortal.

I don't expect God to do something for me that I can do for myself. And there is capacity in health care for prevention, treatment, mitigation, and even the occasional cure. Latter-day Saints make use, hopefully wisely, of medical technology. But when medicine and surgery fail, as they will for every person on earth, I seek the power of God to help me and my fellow men.

Those with the faith to rely on Jesus and the intent to live as He did will be favored through His tender mercy with a spiritual gift to comfort and sustain. And sometimes that gift will be the gift of healing. But the gift of healing is not equivalent to the power to heal because that power is connected to the tree of life, and the way to that tree is known only to God. God will not grant humankind a power that we, in our anguish and ambition, may misuse and thereby destroy our chance to receive His greatest gift of eternal life.

GOD IS WITH US
HIS PURPOSES FAIL NOT

P eople can be inspired by the life of Jesus and by what He said without believing that He is the Christ. I know that, and yet I can't help thinking they are missing His whole point.

Isaiah prophesied of Immanuel, or the God who will be with us. Nephi included that prophecy in his own writings, saying about Immanuel, "Butter and honey shall he eat, that he may know to refuse the evil and to choose the good" (2 Nephi 17:15).

I am surrounded every day by evil and good, and sometimes I cannot tell the difference. I know many good people who seem to have good intentions. But they seem to be as prone to confusion as I am. I feel inclined to care about the people around me, to invest in them, and to cling to them. And I want to know that what I do matters to somebody. As my life passes by as if in a dream, I keep reaching out, hoping to take hold of something substantial and permanent. I don't need a few good ideas or to be inspired by wise teachings—I need Immanuel, the God who lived among men and suffered as a mortal but lived for permanence and who was always doing good.

"Hear, O ye heavens, and give ear, O earth, and rejoice ye inhabitants thereof, for the Lord is God, and beside him there is no Savior," wrote Joseph Smith. "Great is his wisdom, marvelous are his ways, and the extent of his doings none can find out. His purposes fail not, neither are there any who can stay his hand. From eternity to eternity he is the same, and his years never fail" (D&C 76:1–4). Why bother orienting your life around something or someone that will fail? Either there is a promise of permanence, or the promise does not really matter to me.

I know God will have a hard time trusting me. I am unholy by my own choice. I have taken the God-given opportunity to choose in this life and used it to separate myself from Him, even though He has clearly stated how to live. By being as I am, all of the good things I seek—including the love I share with the people to whom I cling—can be lost to me forever. I love to be alive, and I want the full experience, using every sensation with a body alert to it all. But I'm not sure I deserve what I want.

Into that uncertainty and separation from God walks a man whom Joseph Smith met and described:

> The veil was taken from our minds, and the eyes of our understanding were opened.
>
> We saw the Lord standing upon the breastwork of the pulpit, before us; and under his feet was a paved work of pure gold, in color like amber.
>
> His eyes were as a flame of fire; the hair of his head was white like the pure snow; his countenance shone above the brightness of the sun; and his voice was as the sound of the rushing of great waters, even the voice of Jehovah, saying:
>
> I am the first and the last; I am he who liveth, I am he who was slain; I am your advocate with the Father.
>
> Behold, your sins are forgiven you; you are clean before me; therefore, lift up your heads and rejoice. (D&C 110:1–5)

God the Father can trust Jesus. Jesus never deserved to be separated from His Father. He lived the way God would have Him live. Jesus came to earth to do the will of the Father, and He did it—every bit of it. God can accept the members of His family Jesus recommends to Him.

I can trust Jesus. He came to earth as a baby who had to grow up as I had to grow up, increasing "in wisdom and stature, and in favour with God and man" (Luke 2:52). He knows all about the confusion of mortality and its suffering, and about the essential unfairness of everything. He knows what it feels like to be separated from God the Father because that happened to Him, too. He understands everything I feel and everything I fear. That's what makes Him the ideal advocate.

Jesus, the God who is with us, means to help us. He means to not just inspire but to lift and preserve the best about us. He has said: "My grace is sufficient for thee" (2 Corinthians 12:9). Through Him, what I achieve can be permanent. By His power I can have life, with full sensation, everlasting.

Jane Austen's epitaph, written by her clergyman brother, expresses my aspirations and reads in part:

> She departed this Life . . . with the patience and hopes of a Christian. The benevolence of her heart, the sweetness of her temper, the extraordinary endowments of her mind obtained the regard of all who know her and the warmest love of her intimate connections. Their grief is in proportion to their affection, they know their loss to be irreparable, but in their deepest affliction they are consoled by a firm though humble hope that her charity, devotion, faith, and purity have rendered her soul acceptable in the sight of her Redeemer. (Epitaph on Austen's tombstone, Winchester)

Jane Austen died just a few years before Matthew Arnold was born. Her constancy in Christianity, chronicled in her epitaph and so discernible in her prose, contrasts with the loss of faith so characteristic of Matthew Arnold's life and that of succeeding generations. From one generation of British literary elite to the next, there was a general shift in modern society away from God and the Son He sent into the world to redeem it. That shift toward godlessness has been calamitous for humankind, a calamity Joseph Smith identified in 1831. Speaking in his prophetic voice as the mouth of God on earth, he said:

> For they have strayed from mine ordinances, and have broken mine everlasting covenant;
> They seek not the Lord to establish his righteousness, but every man walketh in his own way, and after the image of his own god,

whose image is in the likeness of the world, and whose substance is that of an idol, which waxeth old and shall perish in Babylon, even Babylon the great, which shall fall.

Wherefore, I the Lord, knowing the calamity which should come upon the inhabitants of the earth, called upon my servant Joseph Smith, Jun., and spake unto him from heaven, and gave him commandments;

And also gave commandments to others, that they should proclaim these things unto the world; and all this that it might be fulfilled, which was written by the prophets—

The weak things of the world shall come forth and break down the mighty and strong ones, that man should not counsel his fellow man, neither trust the arm of flesh—

But that every man might speak in the name of God the Lord, even the Savior of the world;

That faith also might increase in the earth;

That mine everlasting covenant might be established;

That the fulness of my gospel might be proclaimed by the weak and the simple unto the ends of the world, and before kings and rulers. (D&C 1:15–23)

The calamity is upon us and should be a sufficient stimulus for us to take a new look, with an eye single to God's glory, at the world around us. The commandments given to Joseph Smith and transferred by him and his successor prophets to me are how I know about all this. I am one of the "weak and simple" who has tried to proclaim the fullness of the gospel to the ends of the earth.

Every year in April I make sure to hike several times up to the Bonneville Shoreline Trail from Tomahawk Drive near my home. Along the trail there is a nondescript-looking bush with small yellow blossoms that exude a most remarkable fragrance. For about two weeks every April, that heavenly scent is a gift from God to me. It reminds me of a verse revealed by Joseph Smith in 1831:

The fulness of the earth is yours. . . .

All things which come of the earth, in the season thereof, are made for the benefit and the use of man, both to please the eye and to gladden the heart;

Yea, for food and for raiment, for taste and for smell, to strengthen the body and to enliven the soul.

And it pleaseth God that he hath given all these things unto man. (D&C 59:16–20)

Each spring as I enjoy these blossoms, I feel God's pleasure with His gift to me. But I believe God's pleasure is not limited to the things He created and gave to us. There is, I believe, an underlying sense of gladness within the Restoration of the gospel in these, the latter days. Beyond God's satisfaction with His creation, there is a sense of anticipation associated with this dispensation of the fullness of times.

That anticipation is particularly expressed in the following two scriptures:

Keep all the commandments and covenants by which ye are bound; and I will cause the heavens to shake for your good, and Satan shall tremble and Zion shall rejoice upon the hills and flourish. (D&C 35:24)

And for this cause, that men might be made partakers of the glories . . . the Lord sent forth the fulness of his gospel, his everlasting covenant, reasoning in plainness and simplicity—

To prepare the weak for . . . the Lord's errand in the day when the weak shall confound the wise, and the little one become a strong nation, and two shall put their tens of thousands to flight.

And by the weak things of the earth the Lord shall thrash the nations by the power of his Spirit. (D&C 133:57–59)

What is apparent in these verses and elsewhere in modern revelation is that the renewed work of salvation begun by Joseph Smith will in these last days come to a fruition not ever seen before. We are blessed to live in the dispensation when the kingdom of God will thrive, grow, and never again be taken from the earth. Zion shall rejoice upon the hills, and the weak things of the earth shall thrash the nations by the power of the Spirit.

Every person who fosters in his or her heart a desire to serve God will be called to the Lord's errand. Consider the Lord's errand to be those few things enumerated by the Lord himself in a revelation now known as section 1 of the Doctrine and Covenants:

> That every man might speak in the name of God the Lord, even the Savior of the world;
> That faith also might increase in the earth;
> That mine everlasting covenant might be established;
> That the fulness of my gospel might be proclaimed by the weak and the simple unto the ends of the world. (D&C 1:20–23)

Our errand or calling, if we desire to serve God, is to teach, proclaim, and establish covenants; we must not allow the demands of secular life to distract us from our heavenly purpose.

We live in a time when there is oppression of the poor, mockery of the sacred, denial of revelation, and other great sins—even among those who profess to belong to the kingdom of God. But our prophets are telling us that this is a time of gladness, because this time the kingdom of God on earth is here to stay. Those who will live in gladness will be the weak things of the earth who have prepared themselves for the Lord's errand. They will be bound by their covenants and will thrash the nations by the power of God's Spirit. They will speak in the name of God the Lord, establish His covenant, and proclaim His gospel to the ends of the world. They will do this because they have a desire to serve God and because they cannot be distracted by secular concerns.

Those of us in this day should trust in the Lord God of Israel, cleave unto Him, and depart not from Him. We should yield ourselves unto the Lord. Or, as did the humble Nephites, we should fast and pray, wax strong in humility, become firm in our faith in Christ, and yield our hearts unto God.

If we fail to yield our hearts to God, as Joseph Smith later revealed, we will be called but not chosen "because (our) hearts are set so much upon the things of this world, and aspire to the honors of men" (D&C 121:35) that our minds cannot learn heavenly lessons.

As Christ pointed out, your heart will be where your treasure is (see Matthew 6:21). If what we treasure most is something of this world, if our hearts are set on success with a worldly pursuit, our lives will be spent achieving our secular ambitions. That effort will alienate us from God; we cannot serve two masters.

The process of ridding one's heart of worldly passions requires significant, often painful, effort. As recorded by Joel: "Therefore also now, saith the Lord, turn ye even to me with all your heart, and with fasting, and with weeping, and with mourning: and rend your heart, and not your garments, and turn unto the Lord your God: for he is gracious and merciful, slow to anger, and of great kindness" (Joel 2:12–13).

The blessing of receiving the fullness of the earth that will please the eye, gladden the heart, enhance taste and smell, strengthen the body, and enliven the soul is predicated on exactly this effort: "Thou shalt offer a sacrifice unto the Lord thy God in righteousness, even that of a broken heart and a contrite spirit" (D&C 59:8).

Jeremiah prophesied: "Behold, the days come, saith the Lord, that I will sow the house of Israel and the house of Judah with the seed of man ... so will I watch over them, to build, and to plant, saith the Lord" (Jeremiah 31:27–28). In those days "saith the Lord, I will make a new covenant with the house of Israel, and with the house of Judah. . . . I will put my law in their inward parts, and write it in their hearts; and will be their God, and they shall be my people" (Jeremiah 31:31–33).

We are the people of this prophecy, the people of the new covenant. Of us "the Lord requireth the heart and a willing mind; and the willing and obedient shall eat the good of the land of Zion in these last days" (D&C 64:34).

Yield your heart to God. Fill your heart with the desire to serve God. Rend your heart and turn unto the Lord, for where your heart is, there will your treasure be also. Then you will be made partakers of the glories of the Lord, and your souls will be full of joy and consolation.

Because of what Joseph Smith has taught me, I have been able to speak in the name of God, to have my faith increased, and have entered into an everlasting covenant with my brother, Jesus. Through Joseph Smith there has been a renaissance of religion in the modern world such that I have been able, thus far, to avoid the awful situation of those described by the Apostle Paul who are "without Christ, being aliens from the commonwealth of Israel, and strangers from the covenants of promise, having no hope" (Ephesians 2:12). Joseph Smith introduced me to the God who is with us, whose purposes fail not.

About the Author

Joseph Q. Jarvis is a public-health physician and author of *The Purple World: Healing the Harm in American Health Care*. He has been married more than forty years to Annette Wanlass Jarvis, an attorney, and they reside in Salt Lake City, Utah. Their five children and seven grandchildren are scattered across the United States, requiring a good deal of grandparent travel each year. As a young man, Brother Jarvis served a full-time mission in Austria for The Church of Jesus Christ of Latter-day Saints. Over the years he has been blessed by his callings in the Church as an organist, Sunday School teacher, ward mission leader, Scout leader, high councilor, priesthood quorum leader, ward clerk, and seminary teacher. Brother Jarvis is currently the Primary pianist in his ward, where he recently served as bishop. He also leads tours in the Holy Land, where readers can study discipleship in the literal footsteps of the Savior. When not writing or providing public-health consulting services, you will find him driving his Jeep off-road or playing golf off-fairway.

NOTE TO THE READER

Thank you for reading *What the Single Eye Sees*. My desire has been to share with you the blessings of abundant living accrued through the discipline of Christianity. My effort to follow the path of Christian discipleship is the root cause of everything good in my life. The most interesting and engaging activity in my life, together with my wife, is loving my children, their spouses, and my grandchildren. My professional interests, public health and medicine, are also activities wherein much righteousness can be brought about. Visiting the sick, the least of my brethren, a quintessential Christian good cause, is the source of my ongoing urge to change the way Americans do health-care business. May you, gentle reader, join me as we find that power within to anxiously engage in many good causes.

Please connect with me by visiting my website, www.drjosephqjarvis .com, and signing up for my newsletter and/or sending me a private message.

Made in the USA
Monee, IL
14 December 2019